JOB
for
EVERYONE

OLD TESTAMENT FOR EVERYONE
John Goldingay

JOB

for

EVERYONE

JOHN
GOLDINGAY

WJK WESTMINSTER
JOHN KNOX PRESS
LOUISVILLE • KENTUCKY

First published in the United States of America in 2013 by
Westminster John Knox Press
100 Witherspoon Street
Louisville, KY 40202

First published in Great Britain in 2013 by
Society for Promoting Christian Knowledge
36 Causton Street
London SW1P 4ST

13 14 15 16 17 18 19 20 21 22—10 9 8 7 6 5 4 3 2 1

Unless otherwise indicated, Scripture quotations are the author's own translation.

Maps are © Karla Bohmbach and are used by permission.

Cover design by Lisa Buckley
Cover illustration: @ istock.photo.com

Library of Congress Cataloging-in-Publication Data

Goldingay, John.
    Job for everyone / John Goldingay. — 1st ed.
        p. cm. — (Old Testament for everyone)
    ISBN 978-0-664-23936-7 (alk. paper)
    1. Bible. O.T. Job.—Commentaries.   I. Title.
    BS1415.53.G65   2012
    223'.1077—dc23
                                    2012032914

♾ The paper used in this publication meets the minimum requirements of the American National Standard for Information Sciences—Permanence of Paper for Printed Library Materials, ANSI Z39.48-1992.

CONTENTS

CONTENTS

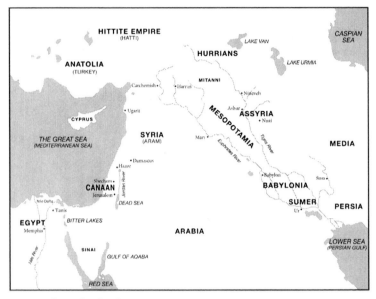

© *Karla Bohmbach*

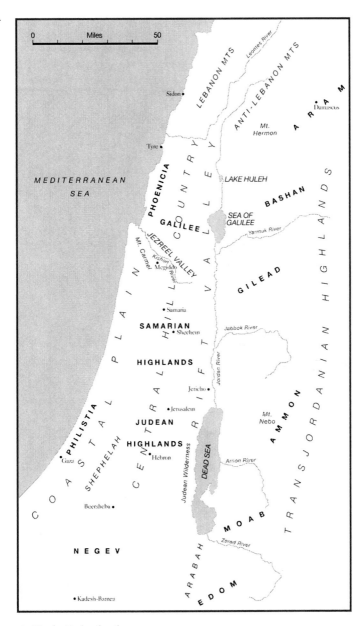

0 Miles 50

MEDITERRANEAN
SEA

Sidon •

Tyre •

LEBANON MTS

Leontes River

ANTI-LEBANON MTS

Mt.
Hermon

A R A M

• Damascus

PHOENICIA

C O U N T R Y

LAKE HULEH

GALILEE

V A L L E Y

SEA OF
GALILEE

BASHAN

Yarmuk River

JEZREEL VALLEY

Mt. Carmel

Kishon
Megiddo
River

H I L L

GILEAD

• Samaria

SAMARIAN

HIGHLANDS

• Shechem

Jabbok River

R I F T

Jordan River

V A L L E Y

Jericho •

• Jerusalem

Mt.
Nebo

A M M O N

JUDEAN

HIGHLANDS

Judean Wilderness

DEAD SEA

• Hebron

Arnon River

T R A N S J O R D A N I A N   H I G H L A N D S

PHILISTIA

• Gaza

C O A S T A L   P L A I N

SHEPHELAH

C E N T R A L

Beersheba •

MOAB

Zered River

NEGEV

A R A B A H

EDOM

• Kadesh-Barnea

© *Karla Bohmbach*

ACKNOWLEDGMENTS

The translation at the beginning of each chapter (and in other biblical quotations) is my own. I have stuck closer to the Hebrew than modern translations often do when they are designed for reading in church so that you can see more precisely what the text says. Thus, although I myself prefer to use gender-inclusive language, I have let the translation stay gendered if inclusivizing it would obscure whether the text was using singular or plural—in other words, the translation often uses "he" where in my own writing I would say "they" or "he or she." Sometimes when I have added words to make the meaning clear, I have put these words in square brackets. At the end of the book is a glossary of some terms that recur in the text, such as geographical, historical, and theological expressions. In each chapter (though not in the introduction) these terms are highlighted in **bold** the first time they occur.

The stories that follow the translation often concern my friends or my family. While none are made up, they are sometimes heavily disguised in order to be fair to people. Sometimes I have disguised them so well that when I came to read the stories again, I was not sure at first whom I was describing. My first wife, Ann, appears in a number of them. Two years before I started writing this book, she died after negotiating with multiple sclerosis for forty-three years. Our shared dealings with her illness and disability over these years contribute significantly to what I write, in ways you will be able to see in connection with a book such as Job but also in ways that are less obvious. Just before I started writing this book, I fell in love with and married Kathleen Scott, and I am grateful for my new life with her and for her insightful comments on the manuscript, which have been so careful and illuminating that

ACKNOWLEDGMENTS

she practically deserves to be credited as coauthor. I am also grateful to Matt Sousa for reading through the manuscript and pointing out things I needed to correct or clarify, and to Tom Bennett for checking the proofs.

INTRODUCTION

As far as Jesus and the New Testament writers were concerned, the Jewish Scriptures that Christians call the "Old Testament" *were* the Scriptures. In saying that, I cut corners a bit, as the New Testament never gives us a list of these Scriptures, but the body of writings that the Jewish people accept is as near as we can get to identifying the collection that Jesus and the New Testament writers would have worked with. The church also came to accept some extra books such as Maccabees and Ecclesiasticus that were traditionally called the "Apocrypha," the books that were "hidden away"—a name that came to imply "spurious." They are now often known as the "Deutero-canonical Writings," which is more cumbersome but less pejorative; it simply indicates that these books have less authority than the Torah, the Prophets, and the Writings. The precise list of them varies among different churches. For the purposes of this series that seeks to expound the "Old Testament for Everyone," by the "Old Testament" we mean the Scriptures accepted by the Jewish community, though in the Jewish Bible they come in a different order, as the Torah, the Prophets, and the Writings.

They were not "old" in the sense of antiquated or out-of-date; I sometimes like to refer to them as the First Testament rather than the Old Testament, to make that point. For Jesus and the New Testament writers, they were a living resource for understanding God, God's ways in the world, and God's ways with us. They were "useful for teaching, for reproof, for correction, and for training in righteousness, so that the person who belongs to God can be proficient, equipped for every good work" (2 Timothy 3:16–17). They were for everyone, in fact. So it's strange that Christians don't read them very much. My aim in these volumes is to help you do so.

My hesitation is that you may read me instead of the Scriptures. Don't fall into that trap. I like the fact that this series

1

includes much of the biblical text. Don't skip over it. In the end, that's the bit that matters

An Outline of the Old Testament

The Christian Old Testament puts the books in the Jewish Bible in a distinctive order:

Genesis to Kings: A story that runs from the creation of the world to the exile of Judahites to Babylon
Chronicles to Esther: A second version of this story, continuing it into the years after the exile
Job, Psalms, Proverbs, Ecclesiastes, Song of Songs: Some poetic books
Isaiah to Malachi: The teaching of some prophets

Here is an outline of the history that lies at the background of the books (I give no dates for events in Genesis, which involves too much guesswork).

1200s	Moses, the exodus, Joshua
1100s	The "judges"
1000s	King Saul, King David
900s	King Solomon; the nation splits into two, Ephraim and Judah
800s	Elijah, Elisha
700s	Amos, Hosea, Isaiah, Micah; Assyria the superpower; the fall of Ephraim
600s	Jeremiah, King Josiah; Babylon the superpower
500s	Ezekiel; the fall of Judah; Persia the superpower; Judahites free to return home
400s	Ezra, Nehemiah
300s	Greece the superpower
200s	Syria and Egypt, the regional powers pulling Judah one way or the other
100s	Judah's rebellion against Syrian power and gain of independence
000s	Rome the superpower

Job

Just after the middle of the Old Testament begins a sequence of poetic books that deal with aspects of everyday life, such as personal relationships, money, love, doubt, suffering, and prayer. It may seem odd that they actually start with suffering (Job) and then move onto prayer (the Psalms), to varied aspects of everyday life (Proverbs), to doubt (Ecclesiastes), and to love (the Song of Songs), but this order reflects the chronological order of the figures they are associated with. The story of Job could make people think his life was set in the era of one of Israel's ancestors, such as Abraham. David is the patron saint of psalmody. Solomon is the patron saint of insight, such as that expressed in Proverbs, the Song of Songs, and Ecclesiastes.

Following the narrative from Genesis to Esther, the story of Job is also a surprise because it does not focus on God's dealings with Israel over the centuries as those books did. Indeed, it makes no reference to the exodus or the covenant or the Torah, or to the prophets or the Day of the Lord. In this respect it indeed belongs with Proverbs, Ecclesiastes, and the Song of Songs. These four books focus not on God's acts in history but on questions about understanding the world and human life and about living our everyday lives. The preceding books, such as Exodus and Deuteronomy, were also concerned with helping us to understand the world and human life and to know how to live our everyday lives, but Job, Proverbs, Ecclesiastes, and the Song of Songs approach these questions in a different way. Instead of appealing to the way God acted in events such as the exodus, they appeal to the way life itself is. They reflect on the nature of everyday human experience. This doesn't mean they leave God out or leave morality out—they assume these are part of human experience. But in order to see how to understand life with God and how to live life with God, they look empirically at how life works. In doing so, Job, Proverbs, and Ecclesiastes often use words such as "wisdom" or "insight" to describe their focus. Thus although the whole Bible is concerned with wisdom or insight, these books are often called "wisdom literature."

There are then two aspects to the way these books portray things. On one hand, they can see that life has regularities and patterns and logic. There are ways in which it normally works. On the basis of such patterns, you can work out how to live your life. But on the other hand, they can also see that human experience does not always fit into these patterns. Sometimes it can seem that there are as many exceptions to the rules as there are experiences that fit the rules. Proverbs and the Song of Songs then concentrate on the rules, on the order that characterizes human life, though they also acknowledge that life is not wholly predictable. Job and Ecclesiastes focus on the experiences that belie the rules, though they also acknowledge the rules.

Job discusses one experience that doesn't fit the rules by telling a story about a man who was totally committed to God yet whose life fell apart through a series of catastrophes but was eventually reestablished. It discusses the questions this kind of experience raises by adopting the form of a play, in which the different characters put forward different insights on how we might understand Job's experience. This device makes it possible to express the different insights without having to claim that just one of them is correct. While some of them may be more or less illuminating in connection with Job's particular story, none of them contains the whole truth, and none of them is wholly wrong.

Although Job's story is set in a period like Abraham's, this of course doesn't mean it was written then. Like many Old Testament books it doesn't give us much concrete indication of when it was written, and many dates have been suggested. The question matters less than is the case with some Old Testament books precisely because the issue it discusses is a perennial human one. As is the case with some other stand-alone books such as Ruth and Jonah, I assume that it is based on a real person's story, though if the book is pure fiction, it would not detract from its importance. The insights it suggests are independent of whether or not it relates something that actually happened. One reason for doubting that it is pure fiction is that a good person having life fall apart, as Job's does, is a common-enough experience, and while such a person having his or her life rebuilt is less common, it does happen. So there is no reason that the story should not be based on a real person. On the other hand, people going through Job's kind of experience do not usually discuss their reactions by speaking poetry, and this alone suggests that some individual's story has become the basis for a discussion of the issues it raises, which are common human questions.

Job is the first Old Testament book that mostly comprises poetry, and it will help the reading of it to be aware of one or two features of Old Testament poetry. First, it commonly comes in lines that comprise about six Hebrew words, though translating these six words regularly requires twice as many words in English. Usually each line will be a complete sentence, but it will divide into two in some way—the second half of the line will restate the first half, or clarify it, or contrast with it, or elaborate it, or simply complete it.

Second, like most poetry, Old Testament poetry is more succinct than Old Testament prose—it tends to leave out the little words that fill out ordinary sentences and make them easier to understand. That characteristic makes it more concentrated and means it requires more work on our part as readers—which sucks us into it and gets us involved. On the other hand, that characteristic also makes it hard to understand, and combined with the fact that the book of Job uses more unusual Hebrew words than other books, it means the book contains more lines that can be understood in more than one way or that are simply puzzling than is the case with other books. So if you compare a number of translations of Job, there are more differences of substance between them than is the case with other biblical books. This doesn't affect the forest, but it does affect the trees.

Third, like most poetry, Old Testament poetry uses imagery—symbols, pictures, metaphors, and similes. "The arrows of Shadday are in me, their poison my spirit drinks up," Job says. "His trust is a spider's house," Bildad says. Images heighten the impact of things that could be said in prose. They also make it possible to say things that one could not say in prosaic language. In reading, we have to stay with the images in order to understand their meaning and to let them have their impact.

JOB 1:1–5

The Man of Integrity

¹There was a man in the country of Uz named Job. That man was upright and straight, submitting to God and turning from evil. ²There had been born to him seven sons and three daughters. ³His possessions included seven thousand sheep, three thousand camels, five hundred yoke of oxen, five hundred donkeys, and a very large staff. That man was greater than all the eastern people. ⁴His sons used to make a feast at the house of each on his day, and send and invite their three sisters to eat and drink with them. ⁵When the days of the feast had made their round, Job would send and sanctify them, and get up early in the morning and make burnt offerings [according to] the number of them all, because—Job said—"Perhaps my children have committed offense and 'praised' God in their heart." In this way Job would act every time.

Seminary chapel this morning focused on a devotional study of Psalm 23 that involved our asking which phrase in the psalm especially spoke to us. The phrase that leapt out for me was "my cup runs over." I have been married for four months, and I love my new wife and my new life. We have just bought a new bicycle and have for the first time cycled to school together; I have a job I love; my two sons and my two daughters-in-law and my two grandchildren in England are doing well; and the sun is shining. Yet now I come to Job, and it reminds me that I have been this way before; forty-five years ago I was newly married with a new life and a job I loved, but my wife had an illness that would eventually disable her and take her life. Your cup can run over, but it can then run dry. (But maybe lightning doesn't strike the same place twice.)

Job's cup runs over. He had a family full of children; his quiver ran over, too, as Psalm 127 might have put it. He had a fantastic number of sheep, camels, oxen, and donkeys. Job is a very big deal indeed. He is the Paul Getty or Bill Gates or John D. Rockefeller of Uz. He would need those seven sons to help him run his estate; he would need the three daughters to help him cope with the social life that would issue from his responsibilities; and he would need a huge staff to oversee his operation.

6

But before telling us about his wealth, the story tells us about his character. First, he was upright, a man of integrity. More literally, he was "whole" in a moral sense, as Noah was and as God expected Abraham to be. There was a simplicity about him. What you saw was what you got. Translations use the word "blameless," but that's misleading because it's a negative word, suggesting the absence of wrong qualities. Indeed there wasn't much about Job that he had to hide, but the word for "whole" or "upright" makes a positive assessment of his character. Further, "blameless" would rather suggest sinless, and Job will later acknowledge that no one is sinless. Indeed, the Old Testament doesn't assume anyone is sinless, but it assumes we are responsible to be upright, to be people of integrity. It's possible for there to be a truthful moral direction to our lives.

Second, Job was "straight." This image overlaps with uprightness. The Old Testament likes to picture life as a walk along a path. Our job is to stay on the straight path and not turn off right or left. Doing the latter counts as waywardness, one of the Old Testament's common images for wrongdoing or sin. God has laid a straight, moral path in front of us, and our task is to walk the walk. Job does so.

Third, Job was submissive to God. This time translations speak of Job's "fearing" God, which can again give a misleading impression. The Old Testament uses the same words for positive submission, reverence, or respect and for negative fear. Sometimes it does refer to circumstances in which people are right to be afraid of God because they have done wrong, but more often it uses the words that can mean "fear" to describe a positive attitude to God. If you want to be a person of insight, the Old Testament declares, this submissiveness, reverence, respect, or awe for God is the beginning or first principle you need to adopt. Indeed, Job 28 will in due course tell us that this submissiveness simply *is* insight. Given that respect for God means doing what God says, it is closely related to uprightness and straightness. God is upright and straight, and we express respect for God by walking in the way that is not only the way God directs but also the way God himself walks.

Fourth and conversely, then, Job was a person who turned away from evil. Once again the phrase suggests the image of walking the right way and therefore avoiding the wrong way. The phrase also further underlines the Old Testament's assumption that attitudes to life and a relationship with God go together. When we read Psalm 23 this morning, I might have dwelt on the phrase "I will fear no evil," which uses this word "evil" to denote evil that happens to me rather than evil that I do. It is neat that both Hebrew and English use the same word for each of these forms of evil. It points toward the assumption that there is a link between them. If you avoid doing evil, you will avoid experiencing evil. God has made the world a place where things fit together thus, in an appropriate way. The Old Testament's use of those other words that describe Job's moral nature make the same point. The words for uprightness and straightness come most often in Proverbs, which promises that the people who are upright and straight are people who will be able to stay on their land; the people who do not do so will lose theirs. The uprightness of straight people guides them to a good destination. **Yahweh** is a shield to people who walk uprightly; people who walk uprightly walk securely (Proverbs 2; 3; 10; 11). "I walk uprightly," Psalm 26 declares; it's on that basis that I can appeal for God's help. That's why respect for Yahweh is the first principle for living a smart life.

Job has proved this to be so. He is a man who couldn't be outsmarted for uprightness, straightness, respect for God, and avoidance of evil. And the beginning of the book shows how his life embodies what happens to a man who puts those principles into practice in his life.

The opening of the book adds one concrete picture of his piety and of the fullness of his cup. There is maybe nothing that gives a parent a greater sense of fulfillment and gratitude than the growth of one's children to a happy and responsible adulthood. In a traditional society there would be an extra dimension to that fulfillment and gratitude because many children died in infancy. Maybe that has happened to Mr. and Mrs. Job, but if so, they have nevertheless had the joy of seeing ten children grow up. They live in their own homes, like David's sons; maybe they are married, though it rather looks as if their sisters are still single. Perhaps the "day" the story refers to, when each of them had a great celebration that evidently lasted more than

8

one day, was each one's birthday. It rather looks as if Mr. and Mrs. Job were not invited to the party; standing aside in this way is another aspect of the experience of having one's children grow up.

Yet your children can never stop being your children, and you can never feel that they are no longer your spiritual responsibility. That is built into the way the Old Testament sees the family, though in Genesis and in Job there is an extra facet to the way things work. There are no priests, and there is no central sanctuary; in effect the head of the family is its priest, and perhaps the implication is that the family's chapel is located in his house. Job has priestly responsibility for his children, and he does not fall down on his responsibility. Suppose the party had involved some accidental infringement of propriety—suppose the menu accidentally included something that was on the list of foods that God said should not be eaten. Or if the sons and daughters were married, it would hardly be surprising or inappropriate if there had been some sexual activity over the days of celebration, and you would then need a cleansing rite before you went to the worship that Job plans for the next day (the **Torah** prescribes such cleansing).

So first Job sees to that need for cleansing by means of a sanctification or purification ceremony, which would deal with any taboos the children had infringed and thus clear the way for the offering of sacrifices the next day; getting up early is then a sign (as it is elsewhere in the Old Testament) of making a special commitment in doing something. The sacrifices would back an appeal to God for forgiveness of any actual sin as opposed to the breaking of taboos. The reference to possible sin is a puzzle. There's presumably nothing wrong with worshiping God in your heart; it's usually assumed that this must be a euphemism for belittling God in the heart (hence I put "praise" in quote marks). In other words, they might have been committed to God outwardly but might have been secretly praying to another god or secretly trusting in their extensive stuff instead of in God. The Old Testament knows how important it is that your commitment to God be inward as well as outward. Job's concern thus shows in another way how committed he is to his family and to God as he seeks to appeal to God in connection with their possible inward sins as well as with outward sins that would be evident to everyone.

JOB 1:6–12

Covenant or Contract?

⁶A day arrived when the divine beings came to present themselves to Yahweh. The adversary, too, came among them. ⁷Yahweh said to the adversary, "From where do you come?" The adversary replied to Yahweh, "From roaming on the earth, walking about on it." ⁸Yahweh said to the adversary, "Have you applied your mind to my servant Job, because there is no one like him on earth, a man upright and straight, submitting to God and turning from evil?" ⁹The adversary replied to Yahweh, "Is it for nothing that Job submits to God? ¹⁰Have you yourself not hedged about him and about his household and about everything that he has, all round? You have blessed the work of his hands, and his possessions have spread through the country. ¹¹On the other hand, do put out your hand and touch everything that he has. If he does not 'praise' you to your face. . . ." ¹²Yahweh said to the adversary, "There, everything that he has is in your hand. Only against him you may not put out your hand." So the adversary went out from Yahweh's presence.

Yesterday the air-conditioning/heating maintenance office called. After we had a big problem with the air conditioning last year, I took out a maintenance contract to try to avoid a recurrence of problems of that magnitude, so I now pay a certain amount per year, and the company comes to check the air conditioning and the heating system. As long as I continue to pay, they will show up twice a year; as long as they show up twice a year, I will continue to send the check. A contract is a mutual, conditional commitment of that kind. It's different from a **covenant**. When my wife and I married a few weeks ago, we made a different kind of mutual commitment. It's not dependent on whether one of us continues to be able to write checks; it's for richer, for poorer. It's not dependent on whether one of us is sick and unable to fulfill all the roles one might

10

expect of a husband or wife; it's in sickness and in health. It's not dependent on the feelings of one or the other person; it's till death do us part. Is God's relationship with us more like a contract or more like a covenant?

The question is raised by the meeting of **Yahweh's** cabinet that the story of Job now reports. I used to think of God as being on his own in heaven, sitting in glorious splendor but in isolation. It was a strange assumption, because the Scriptures make clear from beginning to end that heaven is quite a crowded and busy place. God does not run the world on his own; he has a vast army of aides who are involved in implementing God's will in the world. Nor does God make decisions on his own; like any sovereign power, he has a cabinet that takes part in the making of decisions. The book of Job refers to them as "divine beings," or more literally "sons of God" or "sons of the gods." We need to remember that the Old Testament uses the word for "God" or "gods" in a broader way than we use the word *God*; it uses it to mean something like "supernatural beings." It of course recognizes from beginning to end that there is a difference between Yahweh and other supernatural beings; in our terms, only Yahweh is God. These other "divine beings" or "sons of God" or "sons of the gods" are not God's offspring. In Psalm 2, God can even call the Israelite king "my son." Being God's son doesn't make you divine.

I don't know for certain why God should choose to share the making of decisions and the implementing of them with other heavenly beings, as I don't know why God chooses to use human beings in fulfilling his purpose rather than doing everything himself, though I wouldn't be surprised if it arises out of a delight in sharing responsibility rather than insisting that one does everything oneself. In other words, it's an expression of love. I guess also that in a paradoxical way the awareness that God involves subordinate heavenly beings as God's agents heightens the sense that God is the real King; a king does not do everything himself. The idea that God shares responsibility and rule in this way also has significant explanatory power, like the awareness that God shares authority with human beings. Both heavenly and earthly beings have the capacity to ignore the directions God gives them for the exercise of their power, and that offers part of the explanation of why things go so wrong—in heaven, evidently, and not just on earth.

So this second scene in Job reports what is perhaps a regular meeting of the heavenly cabinet, when God's subordinates come to report on their activities and when the cabinet makes further decisions about what needs to be done. Indeed, the meeting might be one that illustrates the heavenly beings' capacity to rebel against God, because it would be as easy to translate the description of the event as involving their assembling *against* Yahweh.

Certainly there is an aggressive side to the attitude of "the adversary." The Hebrew word for adversary is *satan*, and translations usually use the English word *Satan* to refer to him, but this is another misleading translation. *Satan* is an ordinary Hebrew word for an adversary; it can be used to refer to a human enemy. In the Old Testament it isn't a name; it regularly has "the" on the front of it. In one of the other occurrences of the word to refer to a supernatural being, in Zechariah 3, "the adversary" is again a figure in a court scene in heaven, so it looks as if the word can especially denote someone who is a legal adversary, a kind of prosecuting attorney. This is something like the role that the adversary plays in Job. A prosecuting attorney isn't an opponent of the judge. Both the prosecuting attorney and the defending attorney are present to make sure that the law is upheld. To this end the prosecuting attorney's job is to make the strongest possible case against the defendant, as the defending attorney's job is to make the strongest possible case for the defendant. In Yahweh's cabinet, then, the adversary's job is to make sure that people don't get away with what they shouldn't get away with. In this connection, he is Yahweh's servant. In Britain we refer to the opposition party in parliament as the monarch's "loyal opposition" even though the opposition party is set over against his or her majesty's government. It is being loyal to the monarch by pressing questions about the government's policies to ensure that the government doesn't get away with proposals that have holes in them. The adversary has an analogous role in Yahweh's cabinet.

Of course, the opposition party can get carried away by its opposition to the government, and maybe the adversary can get carried away by his work. Perhaps this possibility explains why the adversary mutates into Satan, the ruler of the kingdom of the air, the great dragon, in the New Testament. But it is worth noting that some New Testament passages imply an understanding of Satan's role that is more like that in Job; the story of Jesus' testing in the wilderness is an example. And conversely, the Old Testament does assume the existence of an entity that embodies direct, aggressive opposition to God, like that of Satan; we will come across this entity in Job 41.

The story in Job 1 safeguards against the danger that God could be too soft. The Old Testament knows that God's instinct, after all, is to be merciful, yet God also has to take responsibility for the moral state of the world and not give the impression that right and wrong don't matter. God is in the position of a mother or father, whose instincts are always to let children get away with things, or the position of a teacher, who wants to give everyone an A. But parents sometimes have to make themselves exercise discipline, and teachers sometimes have to fail people. Otherwise the notion of standards becomes meaningless for children and for students. The adversary's vocation is to press hard questions about what people may be getting away with and to steel God to call on his capacity to be tough and not to give in every time to God's instinct to be merciful. It is God who appoints the adversary to fulfill that role, and it's not who adversary who takes the initiative in the cabinet meeting in raising the question about Job's integrity. It's God who raises the question. The adversary has been out doing his job in checking on things in the world, and God asks him what he makes of Job.

So the picture Job 1 suggests is worth taking note of. Testing is built into the way God created the world and the way God relates to us, as the story of Jesus' testing illustrates (the New Testament generalizes the point in Romans 5 and James 1). The particular test that comes to Job relates to the question of covenant and contract. In effect, the adversary's suggestion is that the relationship between God and Job may be more like a contract than a covenant. Okay, Job is a man of unequaled integrity, straightness, respect for God, and discipline in avoiding evil. But he is also a man of unequaled prosperity. Are these two facts linked in an unhealthy way? Is Job committed to God only because of what he gets out of it? Indeed, is God committed to Job only because of what God gets out of it, because God likes having someone who makes offerings and concerns himself with God's purpose and God's standards in the world? Does the relationship between God and Job involve an unhealthy form of codependence?

JOB 1:13–22

When Life Falls Apart

[13]A day arrived when his sons and daughters were eating and drinking wine in the house of their oldest brother. [14]An aide came to Job and said, "The oxen were plowing and the donkeys were grazing alongside them, [15]and some Sabeans fell and took them, and struck down the boys with the edge of the sword. I alone am the only one who has escaped to tell you." [16]While this man was still speaking, another came and said, "Fire from God fell from the heavens and burnt up the flocks and the boys, and consumed them. I alone am the only one who has escaped to tell you." [17]While this one was still speaking, another came and said, "Some Chaldeans formed three columns and made a raid on the camels and took them, and struck down the boys with the edge of the sword. I alone am the only one who has escaped to tell you. [18]While this one was speaking, another came and said, "Your sons and daughters were eating and drinking wine in the house of their oldest brother, [19]and there—a great wind came from across the wilderness and struck the four corners of the house. It fell on the young people and they died. I alone am the only one who has escaped to tell you." [20]Job got up, ripped his coat and shaved his head, and fell to the ground and bowed low, [21]and said, "Naked I came out of my mother's womb, and naked I will go back there. Yahweh gave and Yahweh has taken. Yahweh's name be praised." [21]In all this Job did not offend. He did not ascribe impropriety to God.

Some years ago I had an eccentric student in a postgraduate seminar, a former Hollywood production manager who lived on a yacht in a nearby marina. After completing a degree he sailed off around the world to distribute Bibles in places where he thought they were needed. Some weeks ago his yacht was hijacked by Somali pirates, who killed him and his wife and another couple. The same weekend, a bus carrying young people from a church in our city that has many links with our seminary crashed in the nearby mountains. The crash killed the driver, injured the other passengers, who included a pastor who is also a student from our seminary, and critically injured the daughter of another student.

How do you react when such things happen? For Job, they happened not merely to people from his community. They devastated his family and his wider household. There are several aspects to his reaction. First, he does not pretend that nothing has happened, that he can sail through tragic experiences unaffected. He gets up from his sitting position and rips his coat and shaves his head in traditional signs of grief and mourning. Then he falls prostrate to the ground. It is the posture you take before someone superior to you, and it is thus a posture you take when you are recognizing that God is God and when you are submitting yourself to God. It is one of the natural postures for worship; in your body you embody the attitude of your will to God.

Now, Job knows that recognition of God needs to be a matter of inner attitude; we have been told that he was aware of the theoretical possibility that his children might have been acknowledging some other god in secret even while they were publicly worshiping **Yahweh**. It was a regular problem in Israel, where people officially belonged to a people that recognized Yahweh but often hedged their bets by secretly praying to other gods. Similarly people in parts of our world may go to church on Sundays but observe other religious practices or trust in their money or their status during the week. Yes, Job knows that inner attitude matters as well as outward observance. But here he shows how he also knows that outward posture matters as well as inner attitude, because we are bodies as well as hearts, and we relate to God with both. He knows instinctively that one cannot worship God sitting down; he can only fall on his face.

Worship is not only a matter of attitude and posture; it involves words. Job's words correspond to his actions. His actions suggest that he is exposing himself in his bare humanness. Ripping his coat takes him half way to being unclothed.

Cutting off his long hair removes one of the marks of his manhood and distinction and turns him back to the way he was when he was born. The tragedies that have suddenly befallen him mean that everything has been taken away from him. He has nothing. (He is exaggerating, because his wife was not among those who died, and she might be entitled to be a bit miffed at his statement, but a man who has gone through such an experience may be allowed a little exaggeration.) He was born naked, and he will die naked. He speaks as if death means returning to one's mother's womb; it does mean returning to the womb of mother earth.

The worship in words then comes in the statement that follows. Yahweh gave; Yahweh has taken. They are expressed as statements of fact, though one might again see them as involving exaggeration, or at least oversimplification. The accumulation of houses, oxen, donkeys, sheep, and camels hardly happened without hard work on Job's part. For that matter, without his involvement (not to say Mrs. Job's) there would have been no children. Yet he recognizes that it is also the case that without God's involvement, none of these would have come into being. Likewise his declaration that God has taken them all away is an oversimplification. Maybe "fire from God" means what it says, though an expression such as "God's fire" often simply means out-of-the-ordinary, unnatural fire (as when we use expressions such as "I had a divine time"—or when insurance companies talk about "an act of God"). But even if the great wind seemed more than merely natural, it was the Sabeans and the Chaldeans who caused much of the damage, and even if Job sees God's agency behind them, he would know that they made up their own minds to undertake their raids.

Job's instinct in attributing all the disasters to God contrasts with many people's instincts. Often we like to let God off the hook of responsibility for what happens by blaming human free will, though we may alternatively blame God for problems that arise when humans use their free will. Job has a bold and rigorous doctrine of divine sovereignty and responsibility. The advantage of such a doctrine is that it can be the basis for prayer. If God is in charge, we can ask God to change things. Job assumes that God is indeed the chair of the heavenly cabinet.

16

Nothing happens without God's agreeing. Job recognizes that God could take away all that he has just as easily as God gave it in the first place. The statement could have been a protest, not an expression of submission. Yet the words that follow remove any ambiguity. Job praises Yahweh's name.

It is noteworthy that the story uses the name Yahweh to refer to God. It did so in reporting the scene in heaven, and it puts the name Yahweh on Job's own lips. This fact raises the question of what people Job belonged to. We don't know exactly where the country of Uz was, but the reference to eastern people suggests Uz was somewhere across the Jordan, beyond the bounds of Israel. In Lamentations 4 it seems that the Edomites live in Uz, which would fit because they live to the southeast of Israel. An association between Job and Edom would be a telling fact because prophets such as Jeremiah and Obadiah refer to the Edomites as if they are a people who have a reputation for being smart and learned. So the setting of the book of Job lies outside Israel, and Job and the other characters in the book are not Israelites. It's thus natural that they don't speak of the exodus, the **covenant**, and so on. The book's attempt to make sense of Job's experience works with the best considerations available to ordinary smart and learned people, who don't know about the exodus and the covenant, or at least don't do their thinking in light of these realities.

A man who lived in Uz wouldn't know about them whether he lived in Abraham's day or in a later period, and he wouldn't have the name of Israel's God on his lips, though the Israelite writing this story would know that Yahweh was the only real God. So if Job was therefore worshiping God, he must have been worshiping Yahweh even if he did not realize it, and so the author puts the name of Yahweh on his lips. In a similar way, the reference to Job's sanctifying his children, the question whether they might have eaten something forbidden, and the allusion to his offering sacrifices will presuppose the kind of instructions about food, purification, and sacrifice that God gave Israel in the **Torah**. The story's audience would know what it was talking about. So the story's use of the name Yahweh and its references to purification and sacrifice hint that setting the story in Uz is a kind of literary device. It is a

17

story designed to help Israelites, people who know they worship Yahweh. Yet it works by not bringing in considerations that would be suggested by the exodus and the covenant making. Maybe the reason is that these events happened a long time ago and don't have so much power for people today. So the story sees what can be done with the question about bad things happening to good people when you don't appeal to the exodus and the covenant. Throughout the book we will find that the truths about Yahweh's relationship with Israel lie under its surface and sometimes plainly poke their head above ground.

Job's words to God suggest that the submission symbolized by his posture is the real thing. He really does submit himself to God. He does not speak in a way that would constitute "offending" God. The Hebrew verb is the one commonly translated "sin," suggesting falling short of God's expectations or failing to act in the way God would require. The offense would be accusing God of acting improperly. Job recognizes that God has the right to decide how to act.

JOB 2:1–8

Skin for Skin

[1]A day arrived when the divine beings came to present themselves to Yahweh. The adversary, too, came among them to present himself to Yahweh. [2]Yahweh said to the adversary, "From where do you come?" The adversary replied to Yahweh, "From roaming on the earth, walking about on it." [3]Yahweh said to the adversary, "Have you applied your mind to my servant Job, because there is no one like him on earth, a man upright and straight, submitting to God and turning from evil? He still holds onto his uprightness. You incited me against him to destroy him for nothing." [4]The adversary replied to Yahweh, "Skin for skin! All that a man has he will give for his life. [5]On the other hand, do put out your hand and touch his bones and his flesh. If he does not 'praise' you to your face. . . ." [6]Yahweh said to the adversary, "There he is, in your hand. Only preserve his life." [7]So the adversary went out from Yahweh's presence and struck Job down with an evil inflammation from the sole of his

foot to the crown of his head, ⁸and he got himself a piece of pot to scratch himself as he was sitting in the midst of the ashes.

My first wife lived with multiple sclerosis for forty-three years. It was after about the first third of this period that the illness started having a lasting effect on her. She found it harder to walk, and she had a tough time working things out and remembering things, and she naturally didn't have the energy for the relationship with me that she had when we were younger. She then lived for more than twenty-five years with the illness taking more and more of a toll. One of my unsettling reflections on that time is that if I had known a third of the way through our marriage how long the process of her increasing disability was going to last, I am not sure I could have coped with the knowledge. Yet the gradual nature of the process gave me time to keep adjusting to new realities. My image for the way this worked is that it resembled weight training (not that I have done weight training!). You learn to lift one weight, and you can't imagine you could lift one that was twice as heavy, but gradually you learn to lift heavier and heavier weights.

So I wonder whether the adversary missed a trick in his plan to show that he could break Job. If he had attacked Job personally at the same time as he attacked Job's estate and his family, maybe the adversary would have had more chance of success. But maybe the muscles in Job's spirit have developed through his first experiences of loss. Notwithstanding my experience in connection with Ann, if his children had become ill and suffered and died slowly, it might have been harder to handle than their sudden deaths were. The scene now is another meeting of the heavenly cabinet; perhaps it meets once a month, like the president's cabinet in my seminary. Once again **Yahweh** invites the adversary to report on what he has seen in fulfilling his task of making sure people do not get away with things they should not get away with and of making sure God's inclination to be merciful and forgiving does not get out of hand. He invites the adversary to agree that Job has proved himself. "Skin for skin," says the adversary. It may constitute an accusation that Job would see his children's skin as worth sacrificing to save his own, or that Job will attack God's person if God allows the adversary to attack Job's person.

You may have thought that God would know the answer to the questions about Job's integrity. Doesn't God know everything? Can't God work out everything without doing experiments? Can't God look into people's hearts? It's actually surprisingly difficult to find passages in the Bible saying that God knows everything and surprisingly easy to find passages that imply God does not. God consults with his cabinet and asks questions, and elsewhere in Scripture God does have surprises. It's certainly true that God can look into people's hearts and run computer projections, but it looks as if God doesn't always choose to do so. Maybe God recognizes that exercising a divine capacity to know everything that we are thinking before we say it would introduce a kind of unreality (not to say boredom) into God's relationship with us. Maybe God likes things to be established out there in public view. God doesn't just play games with us inside God's head and doesn't just imagine what we might do. God lets us be real and show ourselves, show the world, and show God.

There is another question raised by the account of these scenes in heaven. The Bible relates a number of scenes in heaven or other scenes that the authors could not have witnessed, but it usually tells us how the people who describe the scene came to witness it—for instance, God gave them a vision. Like Genesis 1, Job 1–2 makes no statement of this kind, which leads me to think it's more likely the product of human imagination than the result of a vision that the author doesn't tell us about. In this respect it's like one of Jesus' parables. The author knows about God's cabinet and about the adversary and imagines a scene in heaven that might have been the background to Job's story.

Just because the story is imaginary doesn't make it untrue. It would be like C. S. Lewis's fantasy stories about the lion, the witch, and the wardrobe, which are not factual but do embody truths about God and about God's relationship with us. Many people have picked up Lewis's statement that Aslan is not a tame lion but is a good lion and have been helped in their understanding of Jesus. In a parallel way, the account of events in heaven in the book of Job may give us a true account of aspects of the way God runs the world, determining things in a cabinet to which we are not privy and never will be (as Job was not), even though the story is the product of a divinely inspired imagination.

Yet there is an opposite question the account may raise. It can suggest that God relates to Job like a cat playing with a mouse or that God lets the adversary play with Job in that way. Whether or not the account offers a literally factual account of a scene in heaven, does it offer a true account of God's relationship with us? I wouldn't care to think that considerations of the kind that surface in this story lay behind my first wife's forty-three years of living with multiple sclerosis or behind my living with it.

Now, admittedly we will discover that part of the point of God's eventual appearing to Job is to say, "Tough; deal with it," and maybe God would say something of this kind to me (in fact, God more or less did so once or twice). But when we find that Scripture seems to be saying something odd, it is at least worth asking whether this text is the only place where it does so and, if so, whether we are misinterpreting it in some way. And while other parts of Scripture make the general point that God tests us, portray God as involving his cabinet in decision making, and assume that we have an adversary who is not on our side in the way that God is, the details of the story in Job 1–2 don't recur. It would be unwise to base our understanding of God's way of working with us on the basis of one passage. We would never make the mistake of giving a central place in our theology to a motif that occurs in only one passage—such as the millennium—would we? (Answer, in case you didn't work it out: Yes, we do, or at least many people do.)

When Jesus tells parables, we don't base an understanding of their teaching on details that are present just to make the story work, and the opening of Job's story may be there just to make the story work. Even if Job's story did have an event like the scene in heaven at its background, the book implies that most people's stories of suffering do not have such a scene at their background, so the message of the book for us can hardly lie in the scene in heaven. Indeed, we will see that God does not "solve Job's problem" by telling him about that scene; he never knows about it. What the opening of the book does is make it possible to imagine a scenario that could have been behind the story. That is what I think about it on Mondays, Wednesdays, and Fridays. On Tuesdays, Thursdays, and Saturdays I think it is an imaginative story that indicates a true angle on the way a good person's life can collapse. (On Sundays I go to church and then to the beach, if I am lucky.)

JOB 2:9–13

The Silence of Friends

[9]His wife said to him, "Are you still holding onto your uprightness? 'Praise' God and die." [10]He said to her, "You too speak like one of the stupid women. We accept good from Yahweh. Do we not accept evil?" In all this Job did not offend with his lips.

[11]Three friends of Job heard about all this evil that had come upon him, and each one came from his place: Eliphaz the Temanite, Bildad the Shuhite, and Zophar the Naamathite. They met together by agreement to come to express their sorrow to him and comfort him, [12]but they lifted their eyes from a distance and did not recognize him. They lifted their voice and wept. Each one ripped his coat and they threw dirt over their heads, to the heavens. [13]They sat with him on the ground seven days and seven nights with none of them speaking a word to him because they saw that his suffering was very great.

The day my first wife died, we were planning to go to the beach, so I went on my own the next day. This may sound weird, but it seemed to make sense at the time, and when I got home I was glad I had gone, because there were twelve messages on the phone from people who had come to bring me food or just to drop by or who wanted to express condolences, and I didn't want to see anyone. People use up energy, and I didn't have any energy. Other people sent messages on cards and e-mails, too, and at one level I appreciated their doing so, though the messages didn't help me (except the ones that reminisced about Ann, which made me cry but did mean something).

For me, I'm not sure that people coming by and saying nothing, like Job's friends, would have been an improvement, but we will soon see that once these friends start opening their mouths, they never stop putting their feet in them, so in their case silence was better. But both silence and speech can be focused more on the ones who are speaking or being silent rather than on the person they are supposed to be comforting.

Teman was in Edom, as was likely the case with Uz; we don't know where Shuah or Naamah were, but such hints as we have locate them to the east of Canaan. So Job's friends were people from the same region as Job. Like anyone who wants to bring some solace to people who are in pain, they have complicated feelings. They want to express their sorrow to him and for him. Literally, they want to "shake" for him. Their consolation will mean identifying with him and joining with him in the way it would be natural to express grief. They want to empathize with him, and their empathy will find physical expression. They want to share his pain in that bodily way. Their solace will not be just a matter of kind thoughts or words. And maybe their sharing with him in that way will actually bring comfort, because more often than not the Old Testament understanding of comfort is that it involves not words alone but also actions. Ideally these will be actions that do something about the situation that has brought trouble, but at least (in circumstances such as Job's) the action of actually expressing grief in a physical way would show Job that he is not alone and would bring him some relief.

The trouble is that whatever account they have been given of Job's troubles has not prepared them for the sight of him sitting in his heap of ash. He is unrecognizable as the upstanding, noble figure he once was. It draws from them cries of pain and tears. They tear their coats apart, as Job had. They throw dirt into the air in such a way that it falls back on their heads; we don't know the specific significance of this gesture, though it is presumably another expression of grief. And they sit with Job, saying nothing.

There are hints in the account that Job's friends' failing him may start here, when they first arrive in Uz. Why did they need to arrange to meet together before they came to see Job? Was each of them afraid to face him alone? Were they afraid to "catch" whatever affliction he had brought on himself? Did they need to reassure one another that it was okay? Did lifting up their voices and weeping count as "shaking" for him, or are they protesting on their own behalf? It's frightening to witness

23

someone else's suffering. It raises questions about whether the same thing may happen to us. So why did they say nothing to him? Is that the action of a comforter? In Judaism, it's traditional for people closely related to a person who has died to "sit shivah," sit at home for seven (sheva) days of mourning and prayer. Their neighbors and friends will visit them, but it is traditional practice for the visitors not to speak unless or until the mourners initiate conversation. I don't think we know what lies behind that practice, though it might be that it indicates a recognition that the mourners need to be in God's company and that the visitors should not interrupt such communion. For myself, I would be glad for people to be quiet rather than chatter. Perhaps Job's friends are following a custom like sitting shivah as they sit with him for seven days. But if they are, does this mean they are they relating to him as someone who is as good as dead? This would not be much comfort.

Before their arrival, was Mrs. Job broken by the suffering of the man she loves? Can she no longer stand to watch his suffering? Or does she anticipate the conviction that Job's "friends" will express later on: does she assume he must be guilty of some wrongdoing in order to have deserved the calamities that have come upon him? The calamities have come upon her, too, of course. She has lost her children and the possessions that are the family's livelihood. Whatever is going on for her, she brings another temptation to Job. If he "praises" God (that is, reviles God), then he will open himself to God's directly striking him dead or to the community's assuming it should put him to death in God's name for reviling God. So reviling God would be a way of committing suicide or of getting the community to assist his euthanasia. (The Old Testament does not actually say that a blasphemer is to be put to death, though there are one or two occasions when this happens, and one can see it could be a natural assumption, given that the death penalty is laid down for various lesser acts.)

Mrs. Job is behaving as if she were stupid, Job says. She is talking as if she were the kind of woman who had no religious, spiritual, and moral insight, or as if she were an ordinary woman and not the woman that someone like Job would have married. She has started thinking about him or about herself instead of continuing to be someone who respects God and submits to God. In circumstances like the ones that have come to her, it's easy to cease to be that kind of person. Things have previously gone well in your life, and you have been used to taking that experience for granted. This relates to the fact that comfortable Western people fret about "the problem of suffering" more than people who are used to life's being tough. The possibility of suffering scares most of us; we are used to being in control. People who are used to life's being hard find it easier to continue rejoicing in God when particular tough experiences come to them. Good sense, Job assumes, means respecting and submitting to God. Stupidity means declining to do so. Good sense means recognizing the kind of sovereignty of God that the story assumes. God lies behind the good things and the bad things that happen to us. Ironically, Job uses the word for "evil" that God has used. Job has done no evil, but evil has come to him. That's not fair. But he does not say so. (Yet.)

JOB 3:1–26

Perish the Day I Was Born

¹ After that, Job opened his mouth and belittled his [birth]
        day. ²Job spoke out and said:
³ Perish the day on which I was born,
        and the night that said,
        "A male has been conceived!"
⁴ That day should be darkness;
        God above should not inquire about it;
        light should not shine on it.
⁵ Darkness and deathly shadow should reclaim it;
        cloud should settle over it;
        blackness by day should terrify it.
⁶ That night—shadow should seize it;
        it should not join the days of the year;
        it should not come in the count of months.
⁷ There: that night should be barren;
        no shout should come in it.
⁸ The people who curse days should damn it,
        the people ready to rouse Leviathan.

⁹ Its twilight stars should be dark;
  it should look for light, but there should be none;
  it should not see the eyelids of dawn,
¹⁰ because it did not shut the doors of my [mother's] womb,
  hide trouble from my eyes.
¹¹ Why did I not die at birth,
  come out of the womb and breathe my last?
¹² Why did [my mother's] knees meet me,
  or [her] breasts that I would suck?
¹³ Because now I would be lying and still;
  I would have slept then and rested for myself,
¹⁴ with kings and the counselors of the earth
  who build up ruins for themselves,
¹⁵ or with leaders who have gold,
  who fill their houses with silver.
¹⁶ Or [why] was I not buried like a stillborn,
  like babies that have not seen the light?
¹⁷ There the faithless stop thundering;
  there people who are drained of strength rest.
¹⁸ All at once prisoners relax;
  they do not hear the boss's voice.
¹⁹ Small and great are there;
  the servant is free of his master.
²⁰ Why is light given to the sufferer,
  life to the people who are tormented in spirit,
²¹ people who wait for death but there is none,
  who search for it more than hidden treasure,
²² who rejoice with exultation,
  who are glad, because they find the grave?
²³ To the man whose way has hidden,
  and God has hedged him about?
²⁴ Because my sighing comes like food;
  my groans pour out like water.
²⁵ Because the thing I am afraid of happens to me;
  what I dread comes to me.
²⁶ I am not at peace, I am not still;
  I do not rest, thunder comes.

I never knew my Uncle Billy, my mother's younger brother. The
year I was born, he was killed in combat in the Second World

War in North Africa. I did know my Uncle Ray, the husband of my mother's older sister, who was also a combat soldier in that war. He was a quiet, demure man. I associate him with the garden shed where he spent much of his time doing woodwork and creating beautiful things. I remember the time when I was a boy, when someone from the family arrived at our house to tell us that he had hanged himself in his shed. He could no longer live with the memories of what had happened in the war, of what he had seen or of what he had had to do or of what had been done to him.

Job can't live any longer with his memories of the past and with the reality of the present, though the relationship between these is the reverse to my Uncle Ray's. For my uncle, the gruesome realities of the past permanently obtruded on the settled family life of the present. For Job, the gruesome realities of the present stand in horrifying contrast to the settled family life of the past. Both men found the tension intolerable. It doesn't seem that Job contemplated suicide. There are two biblical accounts of suicide (Saul and Judas), and these stories are told without moral comment. They are the tragic end to tragic lives for which both men themselves have to bear responsibility, even though in both cases God's sovereignty is strangely involved in their stories, as is the case with Job. In their own thinking, then the suicides thus make a sort of sense. Job, however, is not responsible for his situation. He was not responsible for beginning his life; he is not responsible for his predicament; and it does not occur to him to take responsibility for ending his life.

What he does do is lament its beginning and long for its end. He calls down a whole sequence of futile curses on the day of his birth. For the most part you do not need me to explain it, as will be the case with much of his protesting through the book. You need to read it, and read it again, and read it again. Maybe I just need to comment on Leviathan; we have already noted that we will gain close acquaintance with this monster figure in chapter 41. Leviathan is one of the Old Testament ways of conceptualizing the concentration and embodiment of dynamic forces that oppose God's positive and orderly purpose in the world. Leviathan is the embodiment of the disorderly, the chaotic, the unruly, the wild, the disruptive, and the violent. It embodies energy that is out of control and focused on destruction. So Job's point here is that Leviathan could be strangely useful, and he imagines the possibility that there are people who are experts in accessing the supernatural who could have gotten Leviathan to exercise its power on the day of his birth. Of course the whole sequences of wishes expressed in verses 3–12 is futile. They are simply unrealistic expressions of his wish that he had never been born. But he was born.

It is more realistic to long for death, as Job does in the second half of the chapter. If he had been stillborn, he could have gone straight from conception to death without enduring life. He knows that the essence of death is rest. The Old Testament has no notion that death may be followed by hell any more than it may be followed by heaven; everyone goes to the same place. It is not a place of suffering or joy but simply a place where nothing much happens. Visibly and physically, it means you go to join the members of your family in the tomb the family shares, and insofar as you have any awareness, you know you are in their company. It is easy to see that death thus means rest. A person may be battling hard as my uncles did, but death means resting. Someone may be fighting an illness, but death means that the person gives up striving and relaxes. A peace can come over the face when that moment arrives; the lines can disappear.

To put it nearer Job's way, a king may be carrying responsibility for a country or an empire, but death means he yields that responsibility. Kings, their counselors, and the other leaders of a country put energy into maintaining edifices from the past that would otherwise be ruins, and/or they set up monumental buildings that are themselves destined to become ruins (because that happens to everything), but all this futile effort ceases when they die. They also cease to be a burden to the people who actually have to do the laboring on their doomed projects and who put in the work that generates the gold and silver that they do not themselves enjoy. Their leaders stop raging at their conscript workers to get them to do their work.

Normally the workers end each day in exhaustion but the next day have somehow to drag themselves to work again. Now they too can rest in death. Yet kings, counselors, and rulers live for a long time (they have better health care and nutrition than the people they govern), and it may be a long time before they die (and anyway they will be replaced by others), so ordinary people and conscript workers can only wait for the rest that will come with their own deaths. Yet death seems never to come. When it does come, they could not be more overjoyed. When my wife died after living with multiple sclerosis for those forty-three years, while I was glad that resurrection day was going to come for her, I was also glad for her (though not for me) that she was now free to rest in the meantime.

Toward the end, Job begins to speak overtly about himself instead of hiding behind the figures of "small and great." He is a man whose way has hidden: that is, he has no future because God has hedged him in (it is the only time he mentions God, apart from the incidental reference in verse 4). He has no way of moving toward a future. He is stuck in this horrible present. The adversary had commented on God's having hedged Job around in a positive sense, but now Job identifies a new hedging. His closing description of himself as characterized by sighing, groaning, fear, dread, and thunder (that is, the roaring trouble that assails him) rather than by peace, stillness, or rest mordantly expresses the nature of his experience as contrasting with everything he finds attractive about death.

While the content of the curse and the protest may seem shocking, the chapter's greater shock lies in the suddenness of the transition from the opening of the story. The expression of such feelings is not what we expect after Job's rebuke to his wife for suggesting he curse God, his declaration about accepting evil from God, or the comment that he did not offend with his lips. Was more going on inside him than those statements indicated? Or is it his friends' silence that has tipped him over the edge? Has he started offending with his lips? Or does his virtually refraining from referring to God or accusing God mean he is still not speaking offensively—that his lament and protest are quite appropriate?

JOB 4:1–21

Can a Mortal Be in the Right in God's Eyes?

¹ Eliphas the Temanite replied:
² If one ventures a word to you, will you be distraught?
    But who could hold back words?
³ Now. You have instructed many;
    you have strengthened weak hands.
⁴ Your words have lifted up the one who was falling;
    you have fortified collapsing knees.
⁵ Because now it comes to you, and you are distraught;
    it reaches you, and you are dismayed.
⁶ Is your submission not your confidence,
    and the uprightness of your life your hope?
⁷ Do be mindful: who is the innocent man who has perished;
    where are the straight people who have disappeared?
⁸ As I have seen, the people who plow wickedness,
    and sow trouble, reap them.
⁹ By God's breath they perish;
    by his angry blast they come to an end.
¹⁰ The lion's roar, the cub's sound,
    the teeth of great lions, crumple.
¹¹ The strong lion perishes for lack of prey;
    the lion's offspring scatter.

¹² A message has been brought to me by stealth;
    my ear got a whisper of it.
¹³ In the uneases that come from visions at night,
    when deep sleep falls on human beings,
¹⁴ fright came upon me, and trembling,
    and it frightened the mass of my bones.
¹⁵ A wind passed over my face
    and bristled the hair on my flesh.
¹⁶ It stood,
    but I did not recognize its appearance,
    the form before my eyes.
    I heard a sound, a voice:
¹⁷ "Can a mortal be in the right before God;
    can a man be pure before his maker?"
¹⁸ If he does not trust his servants
    and attributes folly to his aides,

¹⁹ much more those who dwell in houses of mud,
  whose foundation is in the dirt
  [and which] people can crush like a moth.
²⁰ Between morning and evening they are beaten down;
  without anyone noticing they perish forever.
²¹ Is their tent cord not pulled up from them—
  they die, and without insight?

In the heyday of the charismatic movement in Britain, like many people I used to receive short messages from God from time to time for passing on to other people, and sometimes I used to be given such messages by other people. One of my friends who was a leader in the movement used to say that a third of such messages were significant, a third were trivial, and a third weren't true at all. The first of these thirds, however, was not to be despised. Since I have been in the United States, hardly ever have I been either the means of bringing such messages or the recipient of them. I don't know what to make of that fact. But the other day when talking to someone who had had a hard time in her life over the past decade but had recently found her life taking a positive new turn, I sensed again that God had given me something to say to her. You could have called it a trivial, predictable message, but it indeed came to her as an encouraging message from God.

Eliphaz has a message for Job that has come to him in that fashion. I exaggerate, in that I have not had the kind of unusual experience he describes. For me it is just a sense of having something to say to someone that I would not otherwise have thought of saying and whose significance I do not know until the person tells me how it matches an aspect of his or her situation or need. And if someone backed up a message for me with an account of the mysterious way in which it had come, this account would not actually make me more inclined to take the message seriously. The fact that a spirit was involved in bringing a message does not make it more likely that the message comes from God. The New Testament assumes that there are many deceitful spirits in the world, and Jesus gives a lot of attention to confronting bad spirits. So we have to be discerning and test the spirits, the New Testament says.

It looks as if Eliphaz's experience of a spirit's being involved with him plays a role in convincing Eliphaz that his message comes from God and/or that his recounting this experience will make his message more convincing to Job. Even for Eliphaz, however, the real point lies in the words the spirit brings, not in the experience. But the message turns out indeed to be trivial, or at least commonplace. None of us can be in the right before God, can be pure before our maker, or can avoid (moral) folly. Duh!

Admittedly it is an important theological statement. The Old Testament idea of being "pure" is the one that underlies Job's own concern when he sought to "sanctify" his children after one of their parties. Purity means being wary about things that are inconsistent with God's own nature, such as death and sex and idolatry and oppression. These may seem an odd collection of taboos, because oppression is something morally wrong, and sex is something God made good, and contact with death is something one cannot avoid. They have in common that they are in tension with God's own being, so all required people to undergo purification before approaching God. While you can avoid some of them, you cannot wholly avoid others. None of us can be pure before our Maker.

The Old Testament idea of "being in the right" or "being righteous" or "being just" has behind it the conviction that our relationships with God, with other people, with our families, and with our communities place obligations on us. There is a mutual commitment, and we are under moral obligation to do the right thing by these relationships. Eliphaz's reference to being in the right suggests another link with the opening of Job's story, where after concerning himself with his children's purity he offered sacrifice for them that would constitute an appeal for God to forgive them if at times they had not behaved in the "right" way—if they had not done the right thing by God or by other people.

Supplementing the reference to purity and to being in the right, Eliphaz's closing lines add the third way of describing the inevitability of human sinfulness by speaking of folly. He reminds Job that even God's supernatural servants or aides are capable of folly (maybe the adversary is an example). *Folly* is a different word from the one Job used when he warned his wife about the danger of being stupid, but Job was indicating there that he is aware of this danger. If folly is inevitable in God's supernatural servants, Eliphaz comments, how much more will it apply to earthly beings who are made of mud or clay, of the same humble matter as the rest of the created world, and can die without ever gaining insight?

So Eliphaz's "revelation" that no one can be in the right before God makes an important theological point, but it is one that Job is well aware of. Further, it is a point that is irrelevant to Job's own suffering. While no human being could complain at being treated as a sinner by God and being chastised, nothing Job has done justifies his being treated the way he has been; indeed, he deserves it less than anyone.

Actually Eliphaz has already implied this point, which rather suggests that his words to Job are self-contradictory or that they deconstruct: he has encouraged Job to rely on his submission, his uprightness, his innocence, his straightness. Here, Eliphaz also unconsciously takes up terms that have been used of Job in the introduction to his story; only the word *innocent* failed to appear there. Surely Job recognizes that people with such qualities do not simply perish and disappear. Therefore his having those qualities should be his confidence and his hope. Such confidence then contrasts with the fear that is appropriate to the wayward person, who may look as strong as a lion but is wise to take account of the way his troublemaking will rebound on him when he finds his "house" collapsing. In other words, Eliphaz implies, it cannot be that Job's suffering will last forever. If Job has those qualities, God will bring him healing and restoration.

Eliphaz speaks like the kind of teacher whose insight appears in Proverbs, and it is not teaching simply to be dismissed. Indeed, ironically the story of Job will in due course prove Eliphaz right. God does vindicate Job's submission, uprightness, innocence, and straightness. But God is not doing so at the moment, and it requires some insensitivity to invite Job simply to live in light of the way the future may be expected to turn out and to ignore the reality of the present. Eliphaz is right, too, that coping with experiences that come to us is different from telling other people how to cope with them, though he has not applied that truth to himself.

The King James Bible has another way of translating Eliphaz's key statement: "Shall mortal man be more just than God? shall a man be more pure than his maker?" (v. 17). In fact, that is arguably a more natural way to understand Eliphaz's words. It would then make a different point and suggest that Job has no business raising questions about God's acts toward him. We have to let God be God. With regard to what it means to do right or to be pure, it is God who sets the standards. We cannot pretend to have higher standards than God. We must just accept what God does, knowing it must be right and pure. That would also be an important insight but an insensitive reminder.

JOB 5:1–27

Where Could I Go but to the Lord?

1 Do call—is anyone going to answer you;
    to which of the holy ones will you turn?
2 Because vexation slays the fool;
       passion kills the simple-minded.
3 I myself have seen a fool who was taking root,
       but I immediately declared his estate cursed.
4 His children are far from deliverance;
       they collapse in the gate
       and with no one to rescue.
5 The hungry person eats his harvest,
       takes it into baskets,
       and thirsty people pant after their resources.
6 Because wickedness does not come out from the dirt;
       trouble does not grow from the ground;
7 because a human being is born for trouble,
       and plagues go flying high.

8 Yet I myself inquire of God,
       and before God I set my words,
9 one who does great things of which there is no searching out,
       wonders until there is no numbering,
10 the one who gives rain on the face of the earth,
       sends water on the face of the fields,
11 setting the lowly on high,
       raising the mourners to deliverance,

¹² frustrating the intentions of the shrewd,
   so that their hands do not achieve success,
¹³ capturing the insightful in their shrewdness,
   so that the plan of the clever sweeps away.
¹⁴ By day they encounter darkness;
   at noon they grope as in the night.
¹⁵ And he delivers the needy person from the sword
     of their mouth,
   from the hand of the strong one;
¹⁶ so that there is hope for the poor person,
   and wrongdoing shuts its mouth.

¹⁷ There—the good fortune of the man God reproves;
   so do not reject Shadday's correction,
¹⁸ because he is the one who wounds but binds up;
   he injures but his hands heal.
¹⁹ In six troubles he will save you;
   in seven, evil will not reach you.
²⁰ In famine he will redeem you from dying;
   in battle—from the hands of the sword.
²¹ In the scourge of the tongue you will hide;
   you will not be afraid of destruction when it comes.
²² At destruction and blight you will laugh,
   and you will not be afraid of the animals of the land,
²³ because your covenant will be with the stones
     of the countryside,
   and the animals of the countryside will be
     at peace with you.
²⁴ You will acknowledge that your tent is at peace;
   you will inspect your estate and nothing will be missing.
²⁵ You will acknowledge that your offspring are many,
   your descendants like the grass of the earth.
²⁶ You will come to the grave in old age,
   like the gathering of a sheaf at its season.
²⁷ There—we have searched this out, and it is so;
   listen to it, you acknowledge it for yourself.

The story goes that sometime in the 1930s a Mississippi music teacher and Baptist deacon named James Coats was at the bedside of one of his neighbors, whose name was Joe Keyes. Joe was dying, and James asked him if he knew where he would spend eternity. Joe replied, "Where could I go but to the Lord?" The words stuck with James Coats, and he eventually made it the key line in a song we used to sing when I was a teenager. We didn't really know anywhere near enough about the tough side to life to have a clue what the song was about, but we sang with gusto nevertheless, about our lives here below in this sinful world, unable to afford any comforts, battling to face temptations without giving in—where could we go but to the Lord as a refuge for our souls?

It's a key thought in the second half of Eliphaz's initial words to Job. He begins with an exhortation along these lines as he suggests that in the context of his terrible affliction Job should try prayer. It's a piece of advice that is often tempting to give people who are suffering. While their reaction may be "Oh, I hadn't thought of that," more likely they have tried it or dismissed it. It's easy enough to meet people who believed in God until they lost their job or their house or their two children in a car crash. The suggestion that one should try prayer is then likely to receive the kind of response that I could hardly repeat here. Indeed, you could say that it is exactly what happens when Job responds to Eliphaz in the next chapter.

And maybe it's significant that actually Job has not yet tried praying. We know from the opening of the story that prayer had a prominent place in his life before his series of catastrophes began, but as far as we know he has not prayed since. He has bowed to the ground, which might imply prayer, but the story did not say he prayed. He has talked about God quite a bit, declaring that God should be praised and that we must accept bad as well as good from God, and he has talked about what God should do and has done. But he has not spoken to God. In a sense Eliphaz may be onto something.

Yet it soon becomes clear that Eliphaz's exhortation is meant ironically, perhaps even sarcastically, though there is more than one way of understanding its sarcasm. (My mother used to call sarcasm the lowest form of wit—yes, she would say it in response to my expertise in this form of wit.) "Holy ones" is a term for supernatural beings, the divine aides and servants of God to whom Eliphaz referred earlier, and perhaps his point is that there is no chance that God's heavenly servants are going to come to Job's aid, either because they are fallible and God doesn't trust them, or because Job is fallible and God will not be interested in sending them to relieve Job. Further, another irony in Eliphaz's words (an irony he doesn't know about) is the resonance they set up with the opening scenes in heaven where these divine beings have been present for discussions about Job. They know what is going on. The implication of those scenes would be that God would not send one of the divine beings to bring Job some relief because this would short-circuit the testing project that God and the unwitting Job are involved in. God's hands are tied (because he agreed to tie them).

Eliphaz's reference to vexation and passion suggests that he is indeed concerned that Job's own folly could make it impossible for heavenly agents to come to his aid. Vexation and passion are characteristics Job has shown in his protest about birth and death. In due course Job's friends are going to be more explicit in declaring that Job must have brought his trouble on himself. Here Eliphaz is perhaps already hinting at that conviction, or he may be giving Job another piece of "friendly advice" about what he needs to do, or rather about what he needs to be wary of. Anger or resentment and passion are the qualities of a fool, so Job is in danger of turning into one. And we all know what happens to fools. . . . Eliphaz goes on to remind Job what happens. Eliphaz has seen catastrophe come to a fool, his family, and his farm (just as it has to Job!) and had to conclude that the fool was cursed. It shows that the way things work out for humanity is not random. If we are troublemakers, it's as if we were born to be overwhelmed by trouble and to experience the catastrophic consequences.

Eliphaz goes on to declare how he himself operates as one who knows there is nowhere to go but to the Lord, which may be pastorally wiser than telling someone where they should go. In this connection he speaks of the greatness of God as the one who is involved in making the crops grow, rescuing the lowly, frustrating the wily, and delivering the needy. He then reverts to advice and the promise that things can turn out that way for Job, and he offers Job more biblical truth. God is committed to reproving us and disciplining us, and he fulfills that commitment. As the New Testament puts it, if God were not doing so, it would be as if God were not treating us in the way a father would; it's the way we grow. God would be treating us as if we were bastard children. In making this point, Hebrews 12 goes on to note that loving parents discipline you for a while, but not forever, and Eliphaz makes the same statement about God. In a way he is restating his earlier point: Job has reason for maintaining confidence and hope that has a basis in God's nature as well as in Job's uprightness. Whatever calamities fall, God rescues his children from them.

The only trouble is that Eliphaz's theology looks to be incompatible with Job's experience, but his response is still a first impulse when we meet someone in Job's position. It is also the way we comfort ourselves that life is okay if we meet someone, like Job, who is cursing the day he or she was born. We feel the need to look away when we see such a person, to find another reality; otherwise we are in danger of seeing the scary hopelessness of life (or at least its hopelessness without God's blessing).

Near the beginning of the chapter Eliphaz acknowledges that God does things that are beyond searching out. At the end he tells Job he has searched out the truth and has apprised Job of it. Is he contradicting himself?

JOB 6:1–30

Friendship

¹ Job replied:
² If only my vexation could actually be weighed,
    and people could lift on the scales what has befallen me,
      altogether.
³ Because it would now be heavier than the sand of the seas;
    that is why my words have been wild.
⁴ Because the arrows of Shadday are in me;
    their poison my spirit drinks up;
    God's terrors marshal against me.
⁵ Does a wild donkey bray over grass;
    does an ox bellow over its fodder?
⁶ Is tasteless food eaten without salt;
    is there taste in the juice of a mallow?

7 My appetite refuses to touch;
  these things are like food for when I am sick.

8 If only my request would come about
  and God would grant my hope,
9 that God would show willing and crush me,
  let loose his hand and cut me off.
10 And it would still be my consolation
  (though I would contort with writhing that does not spare),
  because I will not have not disowned the words
    of the Holy One.
11 What strength have I that I should wait;
  what end do I have that I should prolong my life?
12 Is my strength the strength of rocks,
  or is my flesh bronze?
13 In truth, I have no help in myself;
  my success has thrust itself away from me.

14 As for one who refuses commitment to a friend—
  he abandons submitting to Shadday.
15 My brothers betray like a wash,
  like the streams in washes that pass away,
16 that are dark with ice
  when snow piles over them;
17 at the moment when they flow, they [then] come to an end;
  in the heat, they disappear from their place.
18 Caravans divert their route;
  they go up into the wasteland and perish.
19 Caravans from Tema look to them;
  traveling groups from Sheba put hopes in them.
20 They are disappointed, because they had trusted;
  they come to it, and they are disheartened.
21 Because now you have become nothing;
  you see calamity, and you are afraid.
22 Did I say to you, "Give to me,
  out of your resources pay a bribe on my behalf.
23 Deliver me from the hand of my foe,
  from the hand of violent people redeem me"?

24 Teach me, and I myself will be quiet;
  explain to me how I have erred.

²⁵ How painful are straight words—
  but how does reproof from you reprove?
²⁶ Do you devise words to reprove,
  and are the words of a despairing man [to go] to the wind?
²⁷ Would you also cast [lots] for an orphan
  and barter over your friend?

²⁸ But now, show willing, turn to me;
  if I lie to your face. . . .
²⁹ Do turn, there should not be wrongdoing;
  turn, the fact that I am in the right is still intact.
³⁰ Is there wrongdoing on my tongue,
  or can my palate not discern deceptive words?

I dreamed last night that I was at the house of a friend and somehow I had been the person informed that his wife had been killed. I was thus the person who had to break the news to him. Sometimes friendship involves having to say tough things. A friend once accused me of being brusque, and when I protested, he was able to point to a recent occasion that illustrated the point (I am still capable of coming across that way). More recently, another friend told me I really ought to do more self-editing or self-censoring before I speak. More than one friend has said they would rather not be driven anywhere by me because I drive too aggressively.

Just before bidding people to love their neighbor, Leviticus 19 urges them to rebuke their neighbor frankly rather than coming to share their guilt, and Proverbs 27 makes the converse point when it reminds us that the wounds of a friend can be trusted whereas the kisses of a foe should arouse our suspicion. Job knows this is so, and in his closing words he urges his friends to behave like friends, though there is perhaps more than a streak of sarcasm in what he says, as there was in Eliphaz's words. Eliphaz has reminded him that he is a sinner. Okay then, Job says, tell me the nature of my wrongdoing. It is hardly a rhetorical question, since he is in enough pain to want out of it desperately. He does not have the energy for word games. But we know from the opening of the book that Eliphaz will have a hard time specifying Job's wrongdoing, because there isn't much of it. In light of what we are told there, it wouldn't be surprising or inappropriate if Job had a pretty clear conscience—not one that pretended to sinlessness but one that could claim to be a person fundamentally committed to walking God's way. Like Paul's being able to claim that he had fought a good fight, the psalmists also often claim to be basically people who are so committed. They imply that if people who follow God cannot make some such claim, there is something wrong.

So Job commits himself to listening to what his friends have to say, even though being told straight about where he has done wrong will be painful. The trouble is that they rebuke him only with vague generalizations (the "you" through the chapter is plural, so Job is not addressing Eliphaz alone, but Eliphaz is in effect speaking for all three). Their reproofs do not really reprove. They do not even look designed to reprove, for they are too vague. Nor do they take seriously Job's own words; the friends are happy to let them float away on the wind.

Job had begun with some defense of his words. Eliphaz had pointed out that vexation (that is, anger and frustration) and passion (that is, such strong feelings) are unwise. Job's response was to suggest that they have not taken seriously what he has reason to be vexed about. What has happened makes it entirely reasonable for his words to be wild or incoherent. God has attacked him. Would he be making such a fuss if there was nothing to make a fuss about?

Eliphaz has twice talked about hope. A man of faith ought always to be able to live in hope, knowing that God will be faithful to someone who is faithful to God. God is one who makes it possible for the poor or oppressed person to have hope because such people know that God delivers. But these declarations fail to take seriously Job's position as someone under attack from God. It does not mean Job is unwilling to talk about hope, but he has made clear enough that his hope lies in the possibility of finding rest in death, and God is evidently unwilling to fulfill that hope. To put it another way, Eliphaz has urged the importance of going to the Lord; Job has done so, and God will not grant his request to be allowed to die. Job does not want to have to wait much longer for death. At the moment he can still claim to have lived a faithful life, not to have turned his back on God's words about how he should live his life, and not to have yielded

41

to the idea that he should curse God and find death in that way. But he is not sure he can maintain that stance forever.

So he really needs his friends' **commitment**. He does not (he later points out) ask for their money, but he actually asks for something more costly. He appeals to one of the key Old Testament virtues, the Hebrew word often translated "steadfast love" or "constant love." It is a kind of upgraded version of love or faithfulness; it is the Old Testament equivalent to *agapē* in the New Testament. It suggests an unconditioned kind of love, a love that emerges from the one who shows it and is not merely a response to the need of the person to whom it is shown. It is a faithfulness that persists even when the person has forfeited any right to it through failing to manifest faithfulness in return.

Job works with a serious definition of friendship. Friendship implies a mutual commitment. To fail to show such commitment is to fail in your reverence or submission to God. Of course that is so; the **Torah** says that people are to care for their neighbors or friends. The book of Job uses for "friend" the word translated "neighbor" in passages such as Leviticus 19, though evidently Job's "friends" were not neighbors in the sense of people who lived near him. The context in Leviticus makes clear that you do not care for your neighbors only when you are getting on well with them; in effect, we might say, the Torah expects you to care for your neighbors even when they are your enemies. Even if Job had wronged his friends, the Torah would still expect them to show commitment to him. But the wrong-doing is the other way. They behave like a wash or wadi in the desert that flows when there has been rain or when the mountain snows are still seeping through but lets you down in the dry season when you most need water. They look more like people who will sell a friend into slavery or cast lots over a dead man's son in deciding how his debts to them will be met.

Why do Job's friends let him down this way? They see calamity, and it scares them, Job says. If a man can be faithful to God as Job has been, and his life can collapse, is anyone safe? They have to establish that there is some moral reason for his suffering in order to relieve their own anxiety. Otherwise the framework within which they live their lives and think of God also collapses.

JOB 7:1–21

What Are Human Beings That You Pay Them So Much Attention?

¹ Doesn't a human being have hard service on earth,
   and aren't his days like the days of an employee,
² like a servant who longs for evening shadow,
   and like an employee who waits for his wages?
³ Thus I have been allotted months of emptiness for myself;
   nights of trouble have been counted out for me.
⁴ When I lie down, I say, "When shall I get up?"
   but evening drags on,
   and I am full of tossings until morning twilight.
⁵ My flesh is clothed in maggots and clogs of dirt;
   my skin breaks and oozes.
⁶ My days have been quicker than a weaver's shuttle,
   and they come to an end with an absence of hope/thread.

⁷ Be mindful that my life is wind;
   my eye will not again see good fortune.
⁸ The eye that sees me [now] will not behold me;
   your eye will be on me, but I will be no more.
⁹ A cloud comes to an end and goes;
   so the person who goes down to Sheol does not
      come up.
¹⁰ He does not return to his home again;
   his place does not recognize him again.

¹¹ Now. I will not restrain my mouth;
   I will speak in the anguish of my spirit;
   I will lament in the torment of my soul.
¹² Am I the sea or the dragon,
   that you set a watch over me?
¹³ When I say, "My bed will comfort me;
   my mattress will carry part of my lament,"
¹⁴ you terrify me with dreams
   and frighten me with visions.
¹⁵ My soul would choose strangling,
   death rather than [life in] my body.
¹⁶ I have rejected [it], I shall not live forever;
   leave me, because my days are a breath.

43

^{17} What is a mortal man that you make him great
    and that you set your mind on him,
^{18} that you attend to him each morning
    and test him every moment?
^{19} How long will you not look away from me,
    not let me alone until I swallow my spit?
^{20} If I have offended, what do I do to you, you who watch
        over humanity?
    Why have you made me into a target for yourself
    so that I have become a burden to myself?
^{21} Why do you not carry my rebellion
    and let my waywardness pass?
  Because I shall now lie down in the dirt,
    and when you search for me, I will be no more.

I have an odd life compared with many of the people who live in the same city as I do. I never cease being grateful for the fact that I can work at home much of the time and that when I go to the seminary, it is a ten-minute bicycle ride. My life contrasts with that of people I can see first thing in the morning if I look through the kitchen window as I make our first pot of coffee. They start driving down our street soon after six toward the freeway that takes them to their place of employment, many of them setting off early to get a jump on the main traffic flow that will slow to a crawl when they near Los Angeles. They will work there all day, possibly in company and activity that is stimulating and enjoyable, but possibly not, until they join the reverse crawl in the afternoon to get home. They will perhaps be unlikely to have the energy to make their own dinners and will rely on takeout or prepared food, and they will most likely collapse on the sofa in front of mindless television in the hope of unwinding before they repeat the performance the next day.

Job didn't know what that kind of day was like, but he could imagine its equivalent in his culture. Job was the boss of a big outfit, and in a way that put him in a similar position to me in that he could be aware of people whose experience of work was very different from his.

The Old Testament's ideal view of work is that every family has its stretch of land and that they work it together. The men will do their part in the fields plowing and sowing and so on, and the women will do their part in the homestead grinding meal and making bread and so on. The whole is a joint operation in which all the family shares. But sometimes things go wrong for a family, and their activity on the farm does not work out because they are unfortunate, or lazy, or inefficient, and they end up having to work on someone else's land—someone who is luckier than they, or harder working, or more efficient, and who takes over their land in return for supplying them with food. That way, little farms may become big agri-businesses; Job's has apparently done so. It is a process that easily leads to abuses that the Prophets condemn, but Job's story hints that it need not do so if the big successful farmer is also someone with Job's uprightness and submission to God.

If the less fortunate or efficient or hard-working are lucky, the process means they become servants of another farmer, a servitude that in theory, at least, is for a short period of years while they pay back their debt and get themselves on their feet again. The **Torah** has rules to govern this process, and other Middle Eastern peoples had similar rules. If they are less lucky and perhaps have no choice but to resign themselves to working for a master who does not keep such rules and takes them on as employees who get paid by the day, they may have little prospect of ever getting on their feet again. In contrast to Western assumptions, then, the notion of employment arises only when someone's life goes wrong. The ideal is not to have a job but to be involved in your own family business. Selling your labor is seen as a sad idea. Being an employee is worse than being a servant. (The word for "servant" is often translated "slave," but this is misleading. The master does not own the slave, cannot treat him or her as he likes, and is likely under obligation to let the slave go after a period of years. A man such as Abraham's servant who is sent off to find a wife for Isaac is evidently in a permanent position, but he is even more clearly not a chattel slave.)

From his own experience as a boss and from watching what happens in other agri-businesses, Job can observe what life can be like for servants and employees—in his case they are the people the story has referred to as his "boys." You may be

45

grateful to be a servant rather than starving, but it is not the same as your family working together on its own farm. You work all day for someone else, looking forward to nightfall. Worse, you may be a mere employee, working all day just for the moment when you get your pay. Your position parallels that of people in the Western world who are really economic slaves, unable to quit their jobs and go back to the "family farm." They live paycheck to paycheck, terrified of losing their jobs to the point they believe they have no alternative to working in terrible conditions. "Thank God it's Friday," they say. It's not how God created people.

But that reality provides Job with his image for human life as he now experiences it. Indeed, he now feels it's the way human life is by its nature. We work for twenty or forty or sixty years, and then we die. That's it. His image is of a weaver's shuttle, which races back and forth across the loom. It looks as if he chose that image because it enabled him to end with a Hebrew word that happens to have two meanings; it can refer both to a cord or thread and to hope or a hoped-for future. The immediate context makes us think of the weaver's thread and of the way the weaver's work stops when the thread runs out. The broader context make us think of the hope of restoration that Eliphaz has twice encouraged Job to have and the hope of dying that Job has described as his actual hope. The word for hope occurs more than twice as often in Job than in any other Old Testament book, reminding us that people who are in no position to be self-sufficient or self-reliant may be driven to be more aware of the need for hope. But in Job the word for hope usually comes in hopeless contexts. Job is both hopeless and hopeful; he is hopeless about life and hopeful about death, where even God would not be able to find him and impose more suffering on him.

Okay, yielding to vexation and passion can bring ruin to a life, but given the reality of his life and of his apparent prospects, Job has nothing to lose by giving expression to those feelings. For the first time he speaks directly to God, and it is to confront God about the way God is treating him—as if he is an embodiment of dangerous and destructive power that God needs to control or as if God is a poor employer who doesn't know how to treat his employees and turns them into people who are simply longing for their shift to be over. Okay, Job is a sinner, like anyone else, but why do Job's ordinary human offenses matter so much to God? Isn't God supposed to be one who forgives sin? Why does God need to treat Job as if he is someone so important? Not for the last time the irony is that we know the answer to this question, but Job will never know it.

Psalm 8:4 asks, "What is a mortal man that you are mindful of him, a human being that you attend to him?" God made humanity little less than divine, gave us glory and majesty, and put us in charge of the world, his handiwork. Hebrews 2 will take up those words and use them as a lens through which to look at Jesus. It recognizes that the world is not yet subjected to Jesus, but it knows that one day this will be the case. For Job, too, the words declare something that contrasts with how things now are. As he takes up the psalm's words, he reworks them so that they express his different reaction to God's mindfulness and attentiveness, which have different implications for him from the ones they have for the psalmist. God made humanity great and/or made him great, but now God continually tests this representative of humanity. Again there is the irony that we know why God is testing Job, but Job never knew.

JOB 8:1–22

On Learning from the Past

¹ Bildad the Shuhite replied:
² How long will you speak these things?
    The words of your mouth are a strong wind.
³ Does God twist the making of decisions?
    Does Shadday twist what is right?
⁴ If your sons offended against him,
    he sent them off by means of their rebellion.
⁵ If you yourself search for God,
    and seek for grace with Shadday,
⁶ if you are innocent and straight,
    surely he will now arise for you
    and restore your righteous estate.

7 Your beginning may be small,
   but your end will grow very great.

8 Because ask the former generation if you will;
   direct [your mind] to what their ancestors searched out,
9 because we are [of] yesterday, and we do not know,
   because our days on earth are a shadow.
10 Will they not teach you, say to you,
   and bring out words from their understanding?
11 Can papyrus get tall where there is no marsh?
   Can rushes grow without water?
12 While it is still in its shoot form when it is not yet cut,
   it would wither before any grass does.
13 So are the ways of all who put God out of mind;
   the hope of the impious man perishes.
14 His confidence breaks off;
   his trust is a spider's house.
15 He relies on his house, but it does not stand;
   he takes hold of it, but it does not hold.
16 While it may be moist before the sun,
   and his shoot may go out over his garden,
17 while its roots may interweave over a heap,
   may look for a house of stones,
18 when he is eliminated from his place,
   it denies him: "I did not see you."
19 Yes, that is the "joy" of his way;
   from the dirt others spring.

20 On the other hand, God does not reject the upright man,
   though he does not take the hand of the wrongdoer.
21 He will yet fill your mouth with laughter,
   and your lips will shout out.
22 Your enemies will clothe themselves in disappointment;
   the tent of the faithless will be no more.

The other Saturday we were sitting in a restaurant by the ocean, and a woman came to talk to us who is a student at the seminary. This particular beach is an hour away, so I asked her if she lived nearby. She explained that she came here on Saturdays to surf in order to recover from a week of study—I don't think she used the word *recover*, but it was some such expression. It left me thinking, "Why does seminary have such a burdening effect on people that they need to recover in that way?" There are a number of possible answers, which differ from seminary to seminary and from individual to individual, but one answer is that seminary makes people question so much of what they have been taught in churches. They have been inducted into a Christian tradition, a way of understanding the nature of Christian faith—in other words, a way of understanding God, the atonement, salvation, Christian life, and prayer. But in seminary they discover that other students and professors have a different understanding. The tradition they had been taught was a proper part of their security, so having it questioned makes for insecurity and perhaps generates the need for surfing (though going surfing is what would make me feel insecure).

The whole story of Job is a massive raising of questions to which the book does not provide answers; it is about living with questions to which we do not have answers. Bildad is the person who embodies the importance of having a tradition concerning the answers, and his speech reflects the way tradition can give one security in life. If you want to know what to believe, he says, ask the previous generation, ask your ancestors. It's not just a matter of what you believe but of how you live. The musical *Fiddler on the Roof* begins with the image of every Jew as a fiddler standing on the roof, trying to scratch out a tune without breaking his neck. How do you keep your balance? You do so by living in accordance with traditions concerning how you eat and sleep and even how you wear your prayer shawl. Sticking by the community's traditions expresses your devotion to God. The traditions tell you who you are and how God expects you to live. Bildad stands for the way someone else's questioning the tradition makes for insecurity.

Tradition says that life works out in a fair way, and almost everyone lives by this assumption. It would be hard to carry on living on any other basis, and we have noted that in the end the story of Job affirms it. God also affirms it to Eli in 1 Samuel 2: "I honor the people who honor me, but the people who despise me are disdained." Although God both honors and disdains, those words to Eli associate God more closely with the honoring than with the disdaining. God's declaration to Abraham

49

about blessing and cursing in Genesis 12 is similar; there, God is more closely involved in blessing than in cursing. Like a parent, God is not equally balanced between an inclination to bless and an inclination to punish. God's instinct is always in favor of blessing, but God can make himself punish when necessary.

Bildad is more balanced. He is as happy affirming that God is the one who disposed of Job's sons and who does not take the hand of the wrongdoer as he is declaring that God does not reject the upright man. If Job turns to God, suggests Bildad, God will now take action for him and restore his righteous estate. That last phrase is a compressed one. His estate is his house and property, and it is righteous insofar as Job has been running it in the right way—that is, in a way that does the right thing by people such as its servants and its employees as well as the poor, who need its generosity, and the people with whom its produce is traded.

Bildad thus fearlessly associates God with punishment as well as with blessing. He affirms that God does not twist the making of decisions or twist what is right. The Hebrew word for "twisting" or "perverting" could remind people of the word for "waywardness." Both God and humanity are supposed to walk the right way, not to pervert their way. Bildad affirms that God does not do so. And the idea of making decisions in accordance with what is right is one that keeps recurring in the **Torah** and the Prophets. You could say it is central to the Bible's tradition of how relationships and community must function. Many translations have the words "justice and righteousness" here, but the Hebrew words denote more precisely decision making that is fair and proper in light of the relationships to which one is committed. They form a great description of God's personal commitments and of the personal commitments God expects of his people—hence that description of Job's estate as characterized by right relationships. Job is someone who reflects God in the way he exercises leadership. At one level Bildad recognizes that this is so.

Bildad also recognizes that God works out both blessing and punishment indirectly, through the "natural" way life works out. Acts have built-in consequences. This, too, is a tradition with which most people look at human experience. It is the built-in consequence of their own rebellion that will have brought Job's children down, Bildad says. Subsequently, he generalizes the point. Things work with human beings the same way that they work with nature—after all, God is the God of both. The spider trusts in the flimsy, gossamer house that it builds, but such a house gets brushed away. Trusting in oneself or in other deities is like trusting in such a house. Papyrus and rushes don't grow if their roots are not in the right medium—they need lots of water, or they will wither. So a man whose life is not in touch with God withers. Being in the right medium means looking to God, hoping in God, keeping God in mind. For a while someone who puts his trust elsewhere may seem to do really well, like a flourishing plant that extends its shoots beyond the garden to the heaps of stones that lie beyond its borders, but then the plant withers (like much of the growth from the seed in Jesus' first parable in Mark 4). So the place where this man was does not even remember having seen him. That is the so-called joy of this plant's experience; another will grow from its soil. It is on the faithless that Bildad wisely focuses his exposition of the way life "naturally" works. In contrast, God is more directly and more personally involved in the fate of the godly. God will take action and restore him. God will fill his mouth with laughter.

Bildad has learned well from the tradition. All that he says about God's nature and God's way of working with the faithless and the upright is true. His declarations about how the faithful may expect their suffering to be short-lived will be proved true in Job's life. But he offers no recognition that there are exceptions to the tradition's teaching. It applies eighty or ninety percent of the time, maybe, but not one hundred percent. There are wicked people who die happily in their beds and faithful people who experience no restoration. This doesn't make the tradition valueless, but it does make it dangerous. The terrible result of absolutizing the tradition is that one can end up rewriting people's lives when they do not illustrate it. That is what Bildad does near the beginning of his address when he speaks of Job's children.

JOB 9:1–35

The God of Wrath

¹ Job replied:
² In truth I acknowledge that it is so;
   but how can a mortal be [able to prove that he is]
      in the right before God?
³ If he wants to contend with him,
   he does not answer him once in a thousand.
⁴ Insightful of mind and mighty in strength—
   who has been tough with him and come out whole?—
⁵ The one who moves mountains though they do not
      acknowledge him,
   who overturns them in his anger,
⁶ who shakes the earth from its place
   so that its pillars shudder,
⁷ who speaks to the sun, and it does not shine,
   and seals over the stars,
⁸ who spread out the heavens by himself
   and trod on the back of the sea,
⁹ who made the Bear, Orion,
   and Pleiades, and the chambers of the South,
¹⁰ who does great things until there is no searching out,
   wonders until there is no counting.
¹¹ There: were he to pass by me, I would not see him;
   were he to go past, I would not discern him.
¹² There: were he to snatch away, who could make him turn
      back,
   who could say to him, "What are you doing?"

¹³ God does not turn back his anger;
   under him Rahab's helpers bow low.
¹⁴ How much less can I myself answer him,
   choose words against him?
¹⁵ Though I am in the right, I would not answer him;
   I would ask for grace from the one who makes decisions
      in connection with me.
¹⁶ Though I call and he answered me,
   I would not trust that he would give ear to my voice.
¹⁷ He crushes me with a storm
   and wounds me greatly without reason.

18 He does not let me get my breath back
    but fills me with torment.
19 If it is in regard to strength—there, he is mighty;
    if it is in regard to the making of decisions—
    who can bring about a meeting for me?
20 Though I am in the right, my mouth could declare me
        in the wrong;
    although I am upright, it could declare me crooked.
21 Although I am upright, I could not acknowledge myself;
    I could reject my life.
22 It is all the same, that is why I say,
    "He brings to an end the upright and the faithless."
23 If a scourge kills suddenly,
    at the despair of innocent people he mocks.
24 The earth is given over into the hand of the faithless;
    he covers the face of its decision makers—
    if not [he], then who is it?

25 My days have been swifter than a runner;
    as they have fled, they have not seen good fortune.
26 They have gone by like boats of reed,
    as an eagle that swoops on prey.
27 If I say, "I will put my lament out of mind;
    I will abandon my look and be cheerful,"
28 I am afraid of all my sufferings;
    I know that you will not hold me innocent.
29 I myself am found faithless;
    why then should I toil in vain?
30 If I wash with soap
    and cleanse my hands with lye,
31 you would then dip me in a pit
    and my clothes would loathe me.
32 Because he is not a man like me, should I answer him,
    should we come to a decision together.
33 There is no arbiter between us
    who might lay his hand on both of us,
34 were he to remove his club from upon me,
    so that dread of him might not frighten me,
35 I would speak and not be afraid of him,
    because in myself I would not be thus.

We were preparing dinner for people in a homeless shelter on Friday when out of the blue my pastor asked me, "What do you say when people ask you why the God of the Old Testament is so different from the God of the New Testament?" Quick as a flash I replied, "I ask them if they have read either the Old Testament or the New," and he laughed. He was referring, of course, to the idea that the God of the Old Testament is a God of wrath and the God of the New Testament is a God of love. The God of the New Testament, I noted, is one who sends trillions of people to hell, which the God of the Old Testament doesn't do; there is no mention of hell in the Old Testament. Conversely, the Old Testament is the story of the God of love working at his purpose with Israel and with the world, while also showing that you can't mess with him.

Job is getting to be very gloomy about the kind of person God is. He can acknowledge the truth in Bildad's general statements, but Job's problem is that even if you are in the right, even if you are relatively innocent, you can't win your case with God if God won't listen to your case. God can decide things on the basis of his own power and authority to make decisions and not on the basis of listening. In some contexts, God's power is good news; as Bildad has noted, God can use his power to put down the wicked. God can put down supernatural forces of evil, the "helpers of Rahab." This is not the Rahab in Joshua (whose name is spelled differently in Hebrew); the term is another name for what the book of Job has referred to already as Leviathan or the dragon, the embodiment of dynamic, supernatural power asserted against God.

But that capacity is no use to a man like Job whom God is set on ignoring. God could pass near Job as God passed near Moses, but the way things are at present, Job would not be enabled to be aware of God's doing so. Given God's power, all Job can realistically do is plead for grace or mercy (yet that would mean speaking as if he were in the wrong when it is not so). Even if God would let him speak, he does not think God would really listen to him. God holds all the cards, whether one thinks in terms of physical might or of legal power.

Job speaks as if the way he is being treated is the whole truth about human experience and about the way God relates to humanity. If one were in a position to suggest to him that he might be unjustly universalizing from one man's experience and thus speaking unfairly about God, he might grant the point but also suggest that he is doing nothing different from what appears in the theological tradition expressed by his friends. The only difference is that he is putting the emphasis on a set of data different from the one they take notice of. It is intrinsic to their theological position that one starts from the nature of empirical human experience. That is all he is doing. If they want to base theology on experience, then let them do so.

The link between theological generalization and Job's personal experience is implicit in the transition to the last paragraph in the chapter. When Job moves to talking explicitly once more about what has actually happened to him, the transition is only apparent; in reality, all through the chapter he has been talking on the basis of what has happened to him personally. The paragraph also makes a transition from Job's speaking about God while speaking to himself to his speaking directly to God—which in light of what he has said in the bulk of the chapter is risky as well as painful. Whereas he once accepted that we must be content to receive bad as well as good from God, now he can only see bad. It is said that when someone loses a spouse after an illness, initially all one can remember is the tough time at the end of the life of the loved one, but that eventually the closing impression fades somewhat and the happiness of earlier years comes back to awareness. All Job can be aware of at the present is the grimness of his experience. His statement is an oversimplification, and an oversimplification in an unfortunate direction. He can no more look forward to good times than look back to them. He can think about the future but only as a future that will bring more pain and more rejection. He is illustrating a common human inclination to assume that the way things are in the present (good or bad) is the way they will always be, though a moment's reflection establishes that this is not so. Our experience is always changing; indeed, one could argue that change is more prevalent than consistency.

Then for the first time Job imagines the possibility of there being someone to arbitrate between him and God. When people think in terms of a God of wrath, they may then think of

Jesus as mediating between this God and sinners like us. In this connection, God's being wrathful toward us would be something that as sinners we quite deserve. Job does not work within this framework. He knows that he does not deserve to be on the receiving end of God's wrath. Although the Old Testament recognizes that our wrongdoing has an effect on all humanity's relationship with God, it does not think of all humanity as being under God's wrath. God's wrath is reserved for people who really deserve it, like superpowers in their oppressiveness and Israel when it has turned from **Yahweh** to other gods. So Job needs someone to rescue him from the wrath he does not deserve, but he knows this is just a nice theological idea. In reality there is no one to rescue you from God. There is no one who can remove the reality of divine attack and/or the threat of further divine attack, so it is not possible for Job to have a proper argument about what has happened to him.

JOB 10:1–22

On Birth and Death

¹ With my whole being I loathe my life;
    I will let loose my lament for myself; I will speak in the
       torment of my soul.
² I say to God, "Do not hold me as one who is in the wrong;
    tell me what it is over which you contend with me."
³ Does it seem good to you that you oppress,
    that you reject the labor of your hands
    and smile on the plan of
       faithless people?
⁴ Do you have eyes of flesh;
    do you see as a mortal sees?
⁵ Are your days like the days of a mortal;
    are your years like the years of a man,
⁶ that you seek for my waywardness,
    inquire after my offenses,
⁷ although you know that I am not faithless—
    but there is no one who rescues from your hand?
⁸ Whereas your hands shaped me and made me,
    altogether around about, you have consumed me.

⁹ Bear in mind, will you, that you made me like mud
  and you turn me back to dirt?
¹⁰ Did you not pour me out like milk,
  set me like cheese?
¹¹ You clothed me with skin and flesh,
  wove me of bones and sinews.
¹² You bestowed life and commitment upon me;
  your attention watched over my spirit.
¹³ But these things you hid in your heart;
  I know that this was in your mind:
¹⁴ If I offended, you would watch me,
  and not hold me innocent of my waywardness.
¹⁵ If I am faithless, alas for me,
  but even if I am faithful, I cannot lift my head,
  full of disgrace,
  drenched with my humbling.
¹⁶ If [my head] stands high, you hunt me like a lion,
  and again show marvels through me.
¹⁷ You bring new witnesses in front of me,
  increase your vexation toward me,
  changes of troops against me.
¹⁸ So why did you bring me out of the womb?—
  I could have breathed my last, and eye not seen me.
¹⁹ I could have been as if I never was,
  I could have been carried from the womb to the grave.
²⁰ Aren't my days few?
  So leave off, get yourself away from me, so that I may
    look cheerful for a moment,
²¹ before I go (and I will not return)
  to a country of darkness and deathly shadow,
²² a land of gloom like night, deathly shadow without order,
  and it shines like darkness.

Yesterday a girl in her twenties was telling me about the death
of her grandmother a day or two before. Like many people of
her generation, she was very close to her grandmother, and
the loss is a significant one. And yesterday another young
woman within my wife's extended family was in labor with her
first baby, who is to be named after my stepdaughter. It seems
only weeks since we heard that this young woman was going

to have a baby, and we have imagined the gradual growth within the womb that nowadays one can even monitor visually through ultrasound. There is nothing greater than the difference between life and death, yet they can come into strange juxtapositions in our lives.

For Job they come into strange juxtaposition in this chapter. They wrestle for his attention. On one hand, there is the process whereby a baby comes into being in the womb. But that is not how Job speaks of it. He speaks of the process rather as one that God brings about. His coming into being is the result of the laboring of God's hands. Bringing a human being into existence is not a trivial achievement, something God tosses off between coffee time and lunch time or without leaving his armchair. It involves labor. Although Hebrew has ways of referring to the toil, effort, and pain involved in giving birth, it happens not to use the verb that comes here in the way that we use the verb "labor" in English, though later in Job 39 God will use it of the ostrich laboring to lay her eggs. In English the link is suggestive. Just as a mother puts a lot of effort into releasing her baby from the womb (the expression "having" a baby is much too mild!), Job recognizes that God had already put a lot of effort into forming the ostrich's baby in the womb.

Job goes on to describe God as "shaping" and "making" him. God is like a craftsperson, and specifically like a potter shaping a figure out of mud or clay. It was the way God brought the first human into existence in the story in Genesis 2, but God did not then leave humanity and nature to do their own work. God shapes each person who comes into being. It was Job's father who poured out his "milk" into Job's mother so that it then coagulated into a fetus. The imagery reflects the traditional assumption that it is the man's semen that generates the form of the baby, for which the mother's womb provides a home, except that Job turns that physical reality into an image for what God does. One could apply to the physical birth of Job, or that of any baby, the language John 1:13 uses of the children of God, who are born "not of blood or of the will of the flesh or of the will of a man, but of God." In other

58

words, they are born not by a natural process, or as a result of a human decision or a husband's will. Instead, it is as if God provides the semen and the womb.

As birth nears, God continues to be involved in the process, which becomes like weaving or knitting in order to generate skin and flesh, bones and sinew. Outside the womb, the baby's mother is knitting clothes for it; inside the womb, God is also knitting. Through the whole process God bestows life, **commitment,** and attention that watches over not merely Job's body but also his spirit.

Yet that last verb heralds the switch in Job's talk that we have been expecting. In the midst of his life God still watches over him but in a different way. Now God is watching over him in order to catch him out. God now oppresses and rejects the labor of his hands, and the hand that shaped Job is a hand that he wishes he could escape. The life that was God's gift has now become a life that Job loathes. Whereas God shaped Job with clay from the ground, now God is turning Job back into the dirt of the ground. It raises the question why God bothered, why Job could not have gone straight from the womb to the tomb. Though Job has particular reason to ask, "Why did you bring me out of the womb?" it is the question everyone needs to ask, though we may not ask it when things are going our way.

Job's problem is the disparity between the care and effort God put into bringing Job into being and the stance God takes to him now. One would expect that God would smile on the life plans of such a person. If the king smiles on you, you have his favor, and your life works out; so it is with God. Smiling issues in blessing. But God smiles on the faithless rather than on Job (there are no particular faithless in mind; it's another way of saying that God is behaving in an upside-down way). It's as if oppressing Job is good for God, as if God got some profit out of it. It's as if God is short-sighted or has only a limited experience of life, like a human being, and can't see what is in his own interests and/or can't see the real truth about Job as someone who is (basically) upright and straight. Or it's as if God has simply forgotten Job, as if he were a project that went right at first but then failed to maintain God's interest, maybe because Job was so boringly successful.

Indeed (Job speculates as he casts around for some quasi-rational explanation of God's action), it's as if the entire idea of God as a loving creator is false and actually God is a sadist who created Job in order to be able to prosecute and persecute him. In reality, it's not going to make any difference whether Job is faithful or faithless. God has made up his mind how he is going to persecute Job. Job takes to the utmost the extraordinary freedom that it is possible to have in prayer, a freedom to say anything without being struck by lightning, a freedom that may somehow be able to provoke God into a response.

So the poetic description of the process whereby God brings a human being to birth gives way to a more down-to-earth description of death. You could say it is also a poetic description in the sense that it is figurative, but its poetic nature takes a different form. There are no colorful images; there are just a number of ways of describing darkness. It transpires that English is deficient in words for darkness; it is hard to represent the variety of the terms Job uses. Darkness, darkness, darkness, darkness: that is the nature of death. Earlier, Job longed for death because it meant rest. He has now put aside that positive connotation. The one element in the picture that does not relate to darkness, the lack of order, may also point to a reversal of a positive connotation about death. In this life there is an order in which everyone knows his or her place—kings and commoners, servants and masters, small and great. In death there is no order, no social structure.

When you die, the family rolls away the stone from the family tomb, and light shines in for the first time since the last body was put there. Yes, the people there are at rest, but the living members of the family cannot help but notice that their loved ones' bodies have decayed; it as if the bodies have gone back to the earth from which they were made. And when the family rolls the stone back on the mouth of the tomb after putting someone there, darkness descends again, darkness, gloom, shadow, night that fails to give way to day. There you lie. You will never return, Job notes.

JOB 11:1–20

Same Old, Same Old

¹ Zophar the Naamathite replied:
² Should a multitude of words not be answered,
    or should a person of [talkative] lips be treated as in
        the right?
³ Your prattle may silence human beings;
    you may mock, and there may be no one to rebuke.
⁴ You may say, "My creed is pure,
    I have been innocent in your eyes."
⁵ Yet would that God might speak
    and open his lips with you,
⁶ and tell you the secrets of insight,
    because there are two sides to understanding,
and you should acknowledge that God carries some of
    your waywardness for you.

⁷ Can you reach God's profundity
    or reach the completeness of Shadday?
⁸ The heights of the heavens—what can you do?
    Deeper than Sheol—what can you know?
⁹ Its measure is longer than the earth,
    broader than the sea.
¹⁰ If he passes by and takes captive
    and summons [an assembly], who can turn him back?
¹¹ Because he recognizes empty men;
    when he sees wickedness, does he not realize?
¹² A hollow man will get a mind
    when a wild donkey is born a human being.

¹³ If you direct your mind
    and spread your hands toward him,
¹⁴ if there is wickedness in your hand, put it away,
    and do not let wrongdoing dwell in your tents,
¹⁵ because then you will lift your face, free of blemish,
    and be constrained, but not fear.
¹⁶ Because you yourself will put your trouble out of mind,
    you will think of it as waters that have passed by.
¹⁷ Life will be brighter than noonday,
    gloom will become like morning.

61

¹⁸ You will be secure, because there will be hope;
    when you look for security, you will take your rest.
¹⁹ You will lie down and there will be no one to disturb,
    and many will court your favor.
²⁰ But the eyes of the faithless fail;
    escape vanishes from them;
    their hope is a dying breath.

As I write it is Holy Week, and last Sunday we read the passion story from Matthew with its exotic account of tombs opening in Jerusalem so that people came out and wandered around after Jesus' death and in anticipation of his resurrection. It's an eyebrow-raising and perhaps scary story, but it presupposes an important perspective. These are Jewish people who as such belonged to God; Matthew calls them "holy ones," the word often translated "saints" elsewhere in the New Testament. It is the word for people who belong to the church, people who are disciples of Jesus. The implication of the story is that people who have died do not simply go out of existence. Somehow they stay in being. People who belong to God but who die are awaiting a day when they will be raised from death, a day that will come about through Jesus' death and resurrection.

Admittedly, to judge from the Old Testament, they do not realize that they are awaiting that day. As far as they know, death is the end. We have seen in the last chapter how Job certainly knows that in his time nothing like a resurrection is going to happen. When you go to the realm of darkness, you don't return. Only after Jesus' death and resurrection will death become a place that yields up its dead. Zophar makes the same assumption about the finality of death. Near the beginning of his speech he refers to **Sheol,** and at the end he refers to death in its finality. Sheol is a kind of nonphysical equivalent to the physical grave. In the last chapter, Job presupposed how people get put in the darkness of the tomb when they die. The Bible works with more of a unity between the body and the person than Christians usually assume, so it takes for granted that what happens to the body and what happens to the person are closely related. Its writers are aware of the obvious fact that the body continues to exist after death (even if it starts to decompose), but that it is now lifeless. They assume that something similar is true of the person or the soul or the spirit. It also continues to exist, but it is now lifeless, so it can no longer think or remember or give praise.

Further, they will be aware, as we are, that although body and person are closely related, they have a little bit of mutual independence in the sense that while my body may be in a certain place (say, in the classroom), my spirit may be somewhere else (say, with the person I love whom I am meeting after the class). We may be present somewhere in body but not in spirit (one of my favorite songwriters has a line about being on the way to see the woman he loves: his soul is already with her when his body is still an hour away). That fact may be part of what makes it possible to think in terms of the spirits or souls or persons of people who have died being in some sense together, in the place the Old Testament often calls Sheol. But the Old Testament doesn't pretend to know much about Sheol beyond what can be inferred from the fact of death and from what one can see happens to the body, and Zophar refers to that fact. The deep truths about God are "deeper than Sheol," so Job should not assume he can know anything much about them.

Later Jewish thinking speaks of four realms about which we cannot know anything unless God reveals it in a supernatural way. There are the realms that lie above us and below us, and the ones that lie ahead of us and behind us. Ahead and behind us are the future and the past; confusingly for Western readers, Old Testament and Jewish thinking thinks of the future as what lies behind us and thinks of the past as what lies in front of us (though this understanding is more logical than the Western one, since we can in fact see the past but we cannot see the future—life is like rowing a boat). The realm above and the realm below are heaven or the heavens, and Sheol (in the Old Testament) or hell (in later Jewish thinking). In other words, we need a revelation from God about everything except what we can see with our eyes here on earth in the present. (Indeed, the Job story illustrates how we may need a revelation concerning what we are seeing here too, if it is particularly unbelievable or uncomfortable or confusing.)

Zophar presupposes something like this and points it out to Job. He speaks first of the realm above and the realm below, but then of the earth and the sea. Humanity can of course know something about the latter pair but not all about them. They remain partial mysteries. Job, at least, was not in a position to travel to the end of the earth or cross the seas. There is no way he can either act throughout earth and sea or know everything about earth and sea in their vastness. Even more obviously, he cannot act in or know about the heavens in their height or Sheol in its depths. (The way Hebrew poetry works encourages us to assume that in a line like this, both acting and knowing applies both to the heavens and to Sheol.) As Zophar sees it, Job has been talking as if he could gain pretty complete understanding of the way God acts across creation and in the world above and below, but of course he cannot do so. Ironically, he makes a point that will reappear in God's own words when God eventually speaks, as is true of many of the friends' statements. The trouble is that they don't see the implications of their statements.

The further irony in Zophar's words is that although he tells Job he should not pretend to understand the way God acts, Zophar goes on to speak as if he himself does have this understanding. Things are more complicated than Job thinks, he says. There are two sides to understanding. The context may suggest that Zophar means there are two sides to an understanding of God. Job has talked much of God's justice and has spoken as if he is the victim of that justice, whereas he needs to recognize that God is also characterized by mercy and perhaps needs to see himself as the beneficiary of that mercy. God is "carrying" some of his waywardness, accepting responsibility for it by not punishing Job as much as he deserves (!).

On the other hand, while there are some people who are morally hopeless cases, empty people, "hollow" people, and such people are never going to change, Zophar politely allows for the possibility that Job does not belong to that category. Job just needs to turn to God, to turn away from his waywardness, and then God will restore him. He may still have problems, but he need not be afraid of how life will finally work out.

Zophar believes that things are more complicated than Job thinks but not more complicated than Zophar thinks. Insight into God's ways is beyond Job but not beyond Zophar. And this would be fine if Zophar went on to offer Job and us some insight that made us say, "Wow! Yes!" But Zophar does nothing of the sort. All he has to offer is what his friends have said, that God will restore Job if he turns to God. In this sense Job can have hope. The word recurs twice in the closing lines. In contrast to this possibility that is open to Job, there is no hope for the faithless. The implication is that he needs to make sure he does not belong to that category. Otherwise the only hope he will have is a dying breath—literally, a breathing out of breath.

JOB 12:1–25

Sovereignty without Principle?

¹ Job replied:
² In truth you are the people
   with whom insight will die.
³ Yet I have a mind like you;
   I do not fall lower than you,
   and with whom are there not things like these?
⁴ I have been a laughing stock to his friend,
   one calling to God, and he answered;
   a man in the right, upright, is a laughing stock.
⁵ While there is contempt for calamity in the thought
   of the person who is secure,
   [calamity] is ready for those whose foot slips.
⁶ Tents stay at ease for robbers,
   and there is security for people who provoke God,
   people whom God holds in his hand.

⁷ So: nevertheless do ask the animals so that they can
      teach you,
   and the birds of the heavens so that they can tell you,
⁸ or speak to the earth so that it may teach you,
   and the fish of the sea so that they can inform you.
⁹ Who does not acknowledge, among all these,
   that Yahweh's hand has done this,
¹⁰ the one in whose hand is the life of every living thing,
   and the breath of every human being.

¹¹ Does the ear not test words
    as the palate tastes food for itself?
¹² Among the aged lies insight;
    in length of days lies discernment.
¹³ With him are insight and strength;
    to him belong purpose and discernment.
¹⁴ On one hand, he demolishes and it is not built up;
    he locks up a man and he is not released.
¹⁵ On the other, he holds back the waters, and they dry up;
    he releases them, and they overwhelm the country.
¹⁶ With him are strength and success;
    to him belong the person who goes astray and the
        one who leads astray,
¹⁷ he makes counselors go stripped,
    turns decision makers into fools.
¹⁸ He loosens the bond of kings,
    ties a belt around their waist.
¹⁹ He makes priests go stripped,
    overthrows the mighty.
²⁰ He takes away speech from reliable men,
    removes the discernment of elders.
²¹ He pours contempt on leaders,
    loosens the belt of the strong.
²² He reveals mysteries from the darkness,
    brings out deathly shadow into the light.
²³ He lifts up nations and destroys them,
    expands nations and leads them.
²⁴ He takes away the reason in the heads of a country's people
    and makes them wander in a wasteland where there is
        no path.
²⁵ They grope in the darkness where there is no light,
    and he makes them wander like a drunk.

My wife and I were talking about Job the other day, and she told me about two different people in a church to which she had belonged who had given up their Christian faith and left the church when they went through the horrific experience of losing a child in a traffic accident. When I talk with people who have had that kind of experience, they too are inclined to express grieved puzzlement: "Why did God allow it to happen?" The mystery to me is the fact that people ask the question. It implies a different understanding of God from any that I find natural. For me, part of that mystery is the assumption that God has a micromanager relationship with the world. In this connection, the story of Job is the exception that proves the rule. God does not usually manage people's lives in the way God manages Job's. Another aspect of the mystery is the assumption that the world would be a better place and humanity would be better off if God had such a micromanager relationship with the world. The world would then be a place in which nothing tough ever happened and nobody ever had to make responsible decisions (because God would always override irresponsible decisions). One question behind the various puzzlements is, "What does it mean for God to be sovereign in the world?"

We could see this question as an aspect of Job's problem. His friends have now got under his skin, and he confronts them in this chapter. As happened in his previous statement, he will eventually get around to addressing God, but he starts by addressing his friends and by speaking *about* God. The trouble with his friends is not merely their lack of sympathy but their gross air of superiority. They know all the answers!

Often we feel a need to be superior. Not to know the answers is a position of great insecurity. For that reason the friends have to dismiss Job's questions, which are based on the nature of his experience, for it belies their answers. But (Job asks) do they think he is stupid whereas they are so full of insight? He does not stand any lower than they do in this connection. Indeed, the alleged insight of which they are so proud is just commonplace. The kind of thing they say is the kind of thing anyone could say. Further, they have not taken serious account of the basics of Job's story. On one hand, Job has been a man who knew what it was like to live in a close relationship with God. Once again Job summarizes the account that the opening of the story gave us. He is a man who would pray and have his prayers answered; he would call and God would answer. And he is a man who lived an upright life and lived in the right way in relation to God and to other people. But more recently he has been a laughingstock.

I get in trouble for laughing at students when they ask questions. For me, laughing is a sign of affection and appreciation; I try to get them to believe that I laugh because I think they are endearing. But for them, laughter is hurtful. It suggests I am dismissing them and dissociating myself from them. That is the kind of laughter Job aroused in his friends. Laughing at him was a way of distancing themselves from him and maybe making sure that a fate like his did not come to them. They believe that they are immune to calamity; their theology assures them that this is so because they are living upright lives. But they are ignoring the implication of Job's life. Calamity may be about to befall you when you have no reason to expect it and have done nothing to deserve it. It is the opposite fact to another that Job addresses: there are people who have every reason to be fearful of calamity on the basis of the way they live their lives in contempt of God and of other people.

When Job talks about what the animals and the birds know, he speaks as if he is addressing an individual. Along with the "so nevertheless" it suggests he is ironically summing up the kind of thing that "experts" like the friends say, the kind of thing a teacher says to a pupil. Such teachers point out what they see as the most basic insights of life, the kind of things that even the creatures in the natural world recognize and that teachers with the wisdom of age also affirm. God is in control of what happens to us, the traditional teaching says, and God is in a position to be sovereign over what happens on the basis of having the needed discernment as well as the needed power.

In going on to describe God's sovereignty at length, Job continues the irony but takes it in a different direction. The way of offering a description of God that comes in the second half of the chapter would be familiar to people from expressions of praise such as Psalm 104 and reminders of God's nature by prophets such as Amos. In the psalm and here in Job, participles are used to describe God as "the one who..., the one who...." The actual content of the descriptions especially recalls the praise in Psalm 107, which also talks about God's pouring contempt on leaders and making people wander in a wasteland where there is no path, about making fruitful land dry, and about the experience of sitting in darkness and deathly shadow.

In the Psalms themselves, people who are going through terrible experiences do praise God as well as protest their experience and beg God to do something about it. Indeed, you could say that Job did so back at the beginning of the story. So people listening to the book would feel as if they were overhearing Job follow the example of the Psalms. But they would also realize that there is something odd about Job's "praise" compared with those familiar parallels. Prophets and psalmists assume that God's power is harnessed to express faithfulness to Israel, or at least to give Israel what it deserves when it is full of contempt for God and for other people. Job makes no such statements about the way God exercises sovereignty in the world. All Job can see is raw power. In a way it is therefore even more shocking and frightening to declare that God's action is characterized by insight, the capacity to decide what to do and do it. Whether you are the person who goes astray or the person who leads such a one astray, you are within the exercise of God's sovereignty. Whether a nation thrives or declines, God is behind it. In the many circumstances in which leaders lose their power, it is God who takes this power away. But Job can see no moral meaning to the way God does so.

JOB 13:1–28

Will You Just Listen?

¹ Now. My own eye has seen all this;
    my ear has heard and understood it.
² In correspondence with your knowledge, I too know;
    I do not fall lower than you.
³ Yet I myself will speak to Shadday;
    I want to argue with God.
⁴ Yet you are smearers of lies,
    empty physicians, all of you.
⁵ If only you would simply be quiet;
    it would be insight for you.
⁶ Do listen to my argument;
    give ear to the case from my lips.
⁷ Is it for God that you speak unjustly,
    or for him that you speak deceitfully?
⁸ Is it to him that you show favor,
    or for God that you make a case?

⁹ Would it turn out well if he examines you;
   would you fool him as one fools a human being?
¹⁰ He would argue strongly with you
   even if you covertly show [him] favor.
¹¹ Would his majesty not terrify you,
   and dread of him fall on you?
¹² Your reminders are aphorisms made of ash;
   your answers are answers made of mud.

¹³ Be quiet for me, and I myself will speak;
   there will come on me whatever may.
¹⁴ Why do I lift my own flesh into my mouth,
   take my life into my hand?
¹⁵ Yes, he may slay me; may I hope?—
   yet I will argue my case before his face.
¹⁶ This, too, will be my deliverance,
   that an impious person would not come before him.
¹⁷ Listen attentively to my words,
   my declaration in your ears.
¹⁸ Now. I have prepared a case;
   I know that I myself will prove to be in the right.
¹⁹ Who is the one who will contend with me?—
   because then I would be quiet and breathe my last.

²⁰ Yet do not do two things to me,
   then I need not hide from your face:
²¹ Take your hand far from me;
   may terror of you not frighten me.
²² Call and I will be the one who answers,
   or I will speak and you make reply to me.
²³ How many are my acts of waywardness and my offenses?—
   make known to me my rebellion and my offense.
²⁴ Why do you hide your face
   and think of me as an enemy to you?
²⁵ Do you hound a windblown leaf,
   pursue dried-up chaff,
²⁶ that you should write down torments for me
   and make me own the wayward acts of my youth,
²⁷ put my feet in the stocks
   and watch all my ways,
   put marks for yourself on the soles of my feet?

²⁸ And this is a person who wears out like something rotten,
   like a garment that moth has eaten.

This afternoon I was on the phone with a friend who had moved to another city because he believed he had a call to go and work in a tough area there. He had joined a tiny church and had started a coffee bar that might be a meeting place for people and a beachhead for reaching people with the gospel. He wasn't expecting that it would be an immediate success, but he believed that God would go with him and would support him. It didn't work out, however, and he feels that he has been let down by the church, has had no real support from God, and has thus overextended himself. God wasn't there. While he doesn't want to do only the kind of things for which he believes he has the resources in himself, neither does he now feel he can take the risk of doing something for which he lacks those resources. He is arguing with himself and with God and wondering what hope he can have for the future.

Job feels that he has been let down by his friends and needs to confront God, and he too talks about hope. He begins by reaffirming to his friends the conviction that he knows as much about how the world works as they do. Indeed, he implies that he knows more. The long statement of Job's that occupies chapters 12–14 comes at the end of the first round of argument between him and his friends. They have all argued for the same understanding of the way life works: God makes things work out in our lives in accordance with the way we live our lives. But they have argued for this view on differing bases. Eliphaz based it on a message he received supernaturally. Bildad argued for it on the basis of teaching that was handed down from the past. Zophar argued for it on the basis of theological conviction. Job implicitly dismisses them all by pointing out that the kinds of statements he has just been making are things he knows to be true because they are empirically verifiable. You need only to look at the way life is, he says, to see the truth in the statements he has made about the way God operates in the world. He has seen it, and they will be able to see it if they only look instead of basing their understanding on supernatural revelation, or things they have been told, or theological theory.

Their insistence on imposing their perspective on him turns them into smearers of lies, people who fail to tell the truth about God and/or fail to tell the truth about Job (by implying that he must have deserved his suffering—an accusation that will become prominent in chapters that follow). It means they are empty physicians, people whose balm makes the patient worse rather than better. They are people who believe they are seeking to honor God by their teaching, but as they are not telling the truth, they will hardly succeed, and furthermore they will hardly find God pleased. They are blinded by their own explanations.

They would be better off shutting up and listening to Job, who unlike them does know what he is talking about. Notwithstanding the danger he warns them about, Job intends to speak with God. It is at this point that he speaks of hope, though it is hard to be sure what he says. English translations indicate that there are two ways of reading the text here. According to the way you spell one of the words, you could translate the line "Though he may slay me, I have hope in him" (in other words, "My hope in him is going to make me speak, notwithstanding the risk"), or "He may slay me; I have no hope" (which fits the broader context of Job's words about God). I can't make up my mind which is right, and the two spellings appear there in the text as alternatives, so I have translated his words as "He may slay me; may I hope?" which is halfway between the two. As he confronts God, the basis for any hope Job has of escaping with his life is that the very fact of his approaching God is a sign of his innocence. Surely a man who was guilty of the kind of acts the friends suspect would not be so stupid as to think he could fool God.

So Job speaks with God. He has done so before, but the new aspect of his words is the way he confronts God as if they were in court. The further irony here, which is unbeknown to Job, is that the story started as a kind of court case, but one in which Job did not have the chance to take part. Yet his confrontation is then humbler than one might have expected. The two things he appeals to God not to do (more precisely, appeals to God to do) are spelled out in terms of God's withdrawing or holding back the hand that could attack Job as he seeks to speak and (thus) holding back from frightening Job so that he cannot say what he wants to say, confrontational though it may be.

72

What Job asks for are the details on what it is he is supposed to have done to earn the suffering he has gone through. In other words, for the sake of argument (at least), he presupposes the friends' theology and wants to know how his life has earned the treatment he has received. Yet taking this stance must be only for the sake of argument because he introduces it with a renewed statement of his confidence that he will prove to be in the right. God will not be able to do what Job urges. And of course Job is right; God would not be able to lay out accusations that justify the treatment of Job as a gross sinner. Job's position anticipates that of Joseph K. in Franz Kafka's novel *The Trial*, who is arrested although he is not aware of having done anything wrong, never discovers what he is supposed to have done, and is eventually executed. Even a catalog of false accusations would make more sense and make the situation easier to live with than punishment for offenses that are unnamed and of which he is unaware.

Obviously there is a sense in which God has not hidden his face at all, as Job goes on to say. God is paying all too much attention to Job. But talk of a face shining or a face hiding is a Hebrew way of describing God's blessing or withholding blessing. It's like the sun shining or hiding. Thus the priestly blessing (Numbers 6) expresses a prayer that God may make his face shine on us and be gracious to us, that God may turn his face to us and make things go well for us. In chapter 10 Job has complained at the way God smiles at the faithless. In contrast, God's face is turned away from Job. Job's position becomes more and more hopeless, but God simply harries him more. We might assume that more attention from God is bound to be a good thing for us, but it is not necessarily so.

JOB 14:1–22

In the Midst of Life We Are in Death

1 A human being, born of a woman,
    is short in days and full of thunder.
2 Like a flower, he comes up but withers,
    flees like a shadow and does not endure.

73

³ Yes, at such a person you open your eye,
   and you bring me for the making of a decision with you;
⁴ who can bring clean from defiled?—
   no one.
⁵ If his days are determined,
   [if] the number of his months is with you,
   [if] you have set his limits and he cannot pass [them],
⁶ turn away from him so that he may cease,
   until he is satisfied with his day, like an employee.

⁷ Because there is hope for a tree;
   if it is cut down, it can renew itself again—
   its sucker does not cease.
⁸ If its root grows old in the earth
   and its stump dies in the dirt,
⁹ at the scent of water it will bud
   and produce shoots like a plant.
¹⁰ But a man—he dies and is prostrate;
   a human being breathes his last, and where is he?
¹¹ The waters fail from a sea,
   a river becomes parched and dry,
¹² and a man lies down and does not rise,
   until the heavens are no longer.
   They do not get up, they do not awake from their sleep.

¹³ If only you would hide me in Sheol,
   conceal me until your anger turns.
   Set a limit for me and be mindful of me:
¹⁴ if a man could die, could he live [again]?
   All the days of my hard service I would wait
   until my renewal comes.
¹⁵ You would call and I would answer you;
   for the work of your hands you would long.
¹⁶ Because now when you would count my steps,
   you would not watch for my offenses.
¹⁷ My rebellion would be sealed up in a pouch;
   you would coat over my waywardness.

¹⁸ Yet a mountain falls, it crumbles,
   and a rock moves from its place.
¹⁹ Water wears away stones,
   its torrents wash away the dirt of the earth,
   and you destroy a man's hope.

 ²⁰ You overpower him forever and he is gone;
      you alter his face and send him away.
 ²¹ His sons find honor but he does not know,
      or they are insignificant and he does not discern it.
 ²² Yes, his flesh hurts him
      and his being mourns for him.

As a pastor, I have been used to reading words from the beginning of Job 14 at funerals, and specifically as the burial party
arrives at the grave with the coffin. The traditional prayer-book
version reads,

> Man that is born of a woman hath but a short time
> to live, and is full of misery. He cometh up, and is cut
> down, like a flower: he fleeth as it were a shadow, and
> never continueth in one stay.

The prayer book words continue,

> In the midst of life we are in death;
> of whom may we seek for succour,
> but of thee, O Lord, who for our sins art justly displeased?
> Yet, O Lord God most holy, O Lord most mighty,
> O holy and most merciful Saviour,
> deliver us not into the bitter pains of eternal death.
> Thou knowest, Lord, the secrets of our hearts;
> shut not thy merciful ears to our prayer;
> but spare us, Lord most holy, O God most mighty,
> O holy and merciful Saviour, thou most worthy Judge
>   eternal,
> suffer us not, at our last hour, for any pains of death, to fall
>   from thee.

These words have disappeared, or at least become voluntary, in
modern prayer books, and I am not sure what I think of that
development. Job expresses a rather gloomy view of what human
life means, and he does so because he is generalizing from his
own experience. To him, human life seems short and full of
thunder—that is, of trouble roaring. Yet it is commonplace that

twenty-first-century people avoid facing the fact that we are going to die, and maybe we need Job's words and those other words that the prayer book adds. As human beings we are indeed like flowers that blossom and then wither. We are no more substantial than a shadow. Whereas a tree that has been felled may sprout new growth, dead men don't rise from the dead, Job notes. It will happen only when the heavens themselves no longer exist. Death is like the drying up of water from an inland sea or the drying up of a river (the analogy may not seem such a good one, because a lake or a river might become full again, though if that happens, it is not because the same water returns).

The question Job raises is why God bothers to show so much interest in such passing, fragile creatures. Are we worth it? Couldn't God just leave us alone? We human beings get defiled by our contact with realities that are incompatible with God's nature (realities such as death and sin). Job once again makes clear that he does not pretend to be totally without sin and defilement. We can do nothing about that defilement, but does God really need to pay attention to us in our defilement? Given that God has fixed the length of human life, couldn't God just leave us alone to live it, like an employee who is allowed to get on with his day and enjoy his work without his boss hanging over him all the time (the employee seems to have become someone who enjoys his work, as he was not back in chapter 7).

Job is implicitly turning on its head the kind of attitude that is expressed in Psalm 8, as he did explicitly in chapter 7. Elsewhere, that is, the Bible would marvel at the fact that God shows an interest in passing creatures such as us. But of course Job is the victim of a different kind of attention.

This fact is reflected in the speculation that follows; one might call it whimsical if his situation were not as desperate as it is. In his first address, Job spoke of death as a place of relief and rest from the troubles of life. **Sheol** is the place all people go when they die, and they stay there forever. But if it is a place of rest and relief, maybe he could go there for a bit of a break before he has to continue his Godforsaken (or rather, God-too-attentive) life? Maybe God could hide him there until the inexplicable divine anger has dissipated? Maybe God is like a mother or father from whom a son or daughter needs to escape until he or she cools down? Maybe God needs a time out, but is it Job who needs to take it? Again Job speaks inconsistently but realistically, in contrast with his address in chapter 7. There, his time on earth is a period of hard service during which he looks forward to death as his release. Here, spending time in Sheol becomes a period of hard service during which he would look forward to coming back to life as his release.

Indeed, Job waxes poignantly lyrical about what this time would be like if it signified that the relationship between him and God were restored to what it had once been. The way the relationship used to work is that God would call out to him and he would answer, like a servant responding to his master in the way Abraham's servant relates to Abraham when Abraham calls in Genesis 24. Our relationship with God is not egalitarian, but it is characterized by intimacy and mutual confidence and commitment. God would long to see Job again. God would again be paying him attention, and not in the negative way God is paying him attention at the moment. Even if he and God would know that he sometimes made mistakes, God would not be waiting to pounce on him as seems to be the case at present. At the moment it seems that God is keeping a careful record of Job's minutest sins (he is not aware of any big ones) in order to make sure of punishing every one of them. Job imagines God exercising the same care to seal up the record into a bag that would thus never be opened. Or it would be as if Job's peccadilloes were placarded on a wall (by someone like the adversary?) but then plastered over by God so that they cannot be noticed.

Yet that's all but a daydream, a flight of the imagination, a reverie, a fancy from cloud-cuckoo-land. In the real world, Job has already affirmed, no one returns from Sheol, and the idea that God will ever again relate to Job in that loving way is a fantasy (when we are desperate, being rational doesn't seem the most important thing; we become open to all sorts of options, even contradictory and irrational ones). First God destroys a person's hope. Then God brings his life to an end (again without wondering too much about consistency, death is bad news once more). One of the things a parent most cares about is the fate of his or her children; but in Sheol there is no knowing of it, any more than of anything else. Pain is all there is as the body is eaten by worms and the spirit grieves for all that is lost. The Old Testament does not see Sheol as a place of suffering, but again Job must not be pressed to be too literal as he projects himself into his future.

JOB 15:1–35

Eliphaz Tries Again

¹ Eliphaz the Temanite replied:
² Would an insightful man reply with tempestuous
    knowledge,
  fill his belly with the east wind,
³ argue with talk that is no use
  and words that have no worth in them?
⁴ Indeed you—you undercut submission;
  you restrain lament before God.
⁵ Because your waywardness teaches your mouth,
  you choose the tongue of the crafty.
⁶ Your mouth declares that you are faithless, not I;
  your lips testify against you.

⁷ Are you the first human being who was born,
  or were you brought forth before the hills?
⁸ Do you listen in God's cabinet,
  or do you restrain insight to yourself?
⁹ What do you know and we do not know it,
  or understand and it is not in our possession?
¹⁰ Among us are both a grey-haired man and an old man,
  mightier in days than your father.
¹¹ Are God's comforts too small for you,
  a word of gentleness to you?
¹² Why does your thinking capture you;
  why do your eyes flash,
¹³ that you turn your spirit on God
  and emit [such] words from your mouth?
¹⁴ What is a mortal that he should be innocent,
  one born of woman that he should be in the right?
¹⁵ There: in his holy ones he does not trust;
  the heavens are not innocent in his eyes.

¹⁶ How much less one loathsome and foul,
   a man drinking wrongdoing like water.

¹⁷ I will explain, listen to me,
   and what I have seen I will recount,
¹⁸ things that insightful people tell
   and have not hidden from their ancestors.
¹⁹ To them alone the land was given,
   and no stranger passed in their midst:
²⁰ All the days of the faithless man, he writhes,
   for the few years that are reserved for the violent man.
²¹ Frightening sound is in his ears;
   when he is doing well, a robber comes upon him.
²² He is not sure of returning from the darkness;
   he is spied over for the sword.
²³ He wanders about for bread, where is it?—
   he knows that the day of darkness is prepared;
     it is ready, at his hand.
²⁴ Distress terrifies him;
   anguish overwhelms him, like a king ready to attack.
²⁵ Because he stretched out his hand against God,
   acted the hero against Shadday.
²⁶ He runs against him head down
   with the thickness of his shields' bosses,
²⁷ because he has covered his face with fat
   and built up brawn on his loins.
²⁸ But he will dwell in ruined cities,
   houses that people do not live in, that have got ready to
     be [rubble] heaps.
²⁹ He will not be rich, his resources will not endure;
   their possessions will not spread over the land.
³⁰ He will not go away from darkness;
   flame will wither his shoots;
   he will go away by the wind from his mouth.
³¹ He should not trust in emptiness,
   leading himself astray, because emptiness will be his
     recompense.
³² Before his time he will wither;
   his branches will not be flourishing.
³³ He will do violence to his unripe grapes like a vine;
   he will throw off his blossoms like an olive tree,

³⁴ because the impious man's gang is barren,
    and fire consumes the tents of the man involved in
       bribery.
³⁵ He conceives trouble and gives birth to wickedness;
    their womb produces deceit.

Today's newspaper contains a long excerpt from a book about a gigantic fraud that brought about the collapse of a Wall Street financial empire during the financial crisis of the first decade of the twenty-first century. The head of the business in question had defrauded investors of billions of dollars. His victims included many charitable and religious foundations and hospitals. The man who devised the fraud had been a prominent, respected figure in the world of finance in the United States. On his exposure and trial, he was sentenced to 150 years in prison. One of his sons, who was allegedly implicated in the fraud, committed suicide; his father describes this as the most awful aspect of the whole affair.

   In any day's news it's not difficult to find evidence for Eliphaz's thesis that wrongdoers get their comeuppance, which he reiterates at the beginning of the second round of debate between Job and his friends. In his previous address, Eliphaz declared that the people who plow wickedness and sow trouble reap wickedness and trouble: their acts rebound on them. In the second half of this present address, he reiterates the point at great length. Much of his focus lies on the inner turmoil of the "faithless" person. Whereas the faithful person is someone who fulfills his responsibilities toward God and toward the rest of the community, by acts such as caring for the widow and orphan and being generous to the needy, the faithless person is the opposite. He is someone who at best ignores such obligations or who at worst takes advantage of the vulnerability of the weak. Eliphaz puts more emphasis on the way the faithless person offends God, portraying it as a matter of deliberate attack like that of a warrior, who has built himself up for the fight so that he is a Goliath-like figure. The two sides to faithlessness are reexpressed near the end of the address in terms of relationships with God as impiety, a don't-care attitude to God (later the word means apostasy), and in terms of relationships with other people as a willingness to work within a culture of bribery, which makes it possible to pervert the decisions of the court and swindle one's way into accumulating land and other possessions.

The consequence of faithlessness on which Eliphaz here focuses is first of all the mental and emotional turmoil it brings. Wrongdoers can never relax. They are always in danger of being found out. They live in fear. Their wealth means they live in danger from people who would rob them. They end up living in places where no one else would live, perhaps because no one else will associate with them or because they take refuge in ruins because they no longer have the resources to live in a proper home. They have to give up their dreams of having so much stuff that it would fill the country.

They bring this fate on themselves. They are like a plant that willfully sheds its grapes or its olives before they get ripe. While the wind from "his" mouth, the hot blast that withers them like grass, might be God's wind, it is a while since Eliphaz has referred to God, so maybe instead he has in mind the picture of faithless people blasting the growth in their own fields. They trust in schemes that are empty, lacking in substance; they themselves are the ones the schemes deceive. They themselves give birth to the trouble and wickedness that rebounds on them.

Yes, this happens, as can be seen in the news item I was relating. The trouble is that for every swindler who gets caught by his own scheme, there seem to be others who get away scot-free, as the story of the financial collapse in 2008 illustrates.

If wrongdoing gets its reward, this fact would be a powerful incentive to right-doing (though it would encourage people to do the right thing for the wrong reason, which T. S. Eliot in *Murder in the Cathedral* describes as "the greatest treason"; but incentives always do so, whether they are positive or negative). Conversely, Job's questioning of Eliphaz's position imperils right-doing. Job's words are dangerous. Thus Eliphaz begins by speaking in terms of their expressing tempestuous (so-called) knowledge that comes from someone possessed by the powerful east wind, who is capable of destroying people in the way he will later describe the faithless as destroying themselves.

Job's words not only lack positive worth, Eliphaz goes on to say; they discourage submission and lament. In other words, they discourage people from living in obedience to God (one of the qualities that we know Job embodied), and they discourage people from praying, specifically when they are in distress and need to protest to God at their circumstances. If Eliphaz's teaching is correct, people have a basis for prayer. If Job's claim that God is not in the habit of doing anything to ensure a correlation between our action and what happens to us, what is the point of prayer? Eliphaz believes that the very way Job talks thus shows that he himself belongs to the category of the faithless.

In the middle of his address, Eliphaz summarizes or refers back to the kind of comment he or his friends have made previously. Job ignores traditional teaching (scriptural teaching, we would say), behaves as if he has a special revelation from God (like Eliphaz himself!), and speaks as if he is the one person in the world who sees straight. Eliphaz had offered Job God's comfort, promising that because he is a person who is basically committed to walking God's way, restoration will come to him. He in essence asks Job, "Is that gentle message not enough?"

JOB 16:1–17

Comforters? More like Troublemakers

¹ Job replied:
² I have heard many things like these;
   all of you are troublesome comforters.
³ Is there a limit to tempestuous words—
   what ails you that you reply?
⁴ I too could speak like you
   if you yourselves were in my own place.
   I could converse with you in words
   and nod over you with my head.
⁵ I could fortify you with my speech;
   the moving of my lips could relieve.

⁶ If I speak, my pain does not find relief;
   if I refrain, what goes from me?

⁷ Indeed he has now worn me out;
  you have devastated my whole community.
⁸ You have shriveled me,
    it has become a witness;
  my gauntness rises up against me;
    it testifies against me.
⁹ His anger has torn and been hostile to me;
    he has gnashed his teeth at me; my foe sharpens his eyes
      toward me.
¹⁰ People gape at me with their mouth,
    with reproach they strike me on the cheek;
    they mass together against me.
¹¹ God has delivered me up to an evildoer,
    has thrown me into the hands of the faithless.
¹² I was at peace, but he has shattered me;
    he has seized me by the neck and smashed me.
  He has set me up as his target;
¹³   his archers have surrounded me.
  He has pierced my kidneys and not spared;
    he has poured my bile on the earth.
¹⁴ He has assaulted me, with assault on top of assault;
    he has run at me like a warrior.
¹⁵ I have sewed sackcloth over my skin
    and buried my horn in the dirt.
¹⁶ My face is red from weeping
    and over my eyes is deathly shadow,
¹⁷ although there was no violence in my hands
    and my prayer was pure.

When I take students through the book of Job in classes, I invite them to let me know the questions it raises for them, and usually someone asks, "So when we are ministering to people who are suffering like Job, what do we say to them if we want to avoid the mistakes of Job's friends?" My response is that the book of Job has no answer to that question, nor is there much of an answer anywhere else in the Bible. That fact has a couple of implications. One is to raise the question of why we think we need to have something to say. The other is that there isn't much that is useful to say. Words aren't much use to people when they are going through Job's experience. A friend of mine who is an alcoholic told me about a woman at an AA meeting who said that she was full of shame from having left her husband for another man and that the best thing anyone ever did for her was to come and stand next to her at an AA meeting—just stand there, nothing else. Sometimes standing next to someone may be the only thing and the best thing to do.

So Job here begins with a wearied complaint about the kind of thing that Eliphaz has just said, which is also the kind of thing that he had said at the beginning and the kind of thing Bildad and Zophar have said. Its theme is that God is fair and that we can trust God to treat us fairly, even when it doesn't seem that God is doing so. The problem is that Job's experience does not match this claim, and we know from the beginning of the book that Job is right in his assessment; the basis for treating Job the way he has been treated was not that God was being fair. It is precisely because Job deserves to be treated well on the basis of the principle of fairness that God is not treating Job well or fairly. We know this is so, but neither Job nor his friends do. The problem with his friends is that they continue to mouth those truths that may work out much of the time but do not work all the time. And Job has heard it all before.

Hearing what theologians have had to say many times before could simply make the theologians boring, but when they are trying to speak to one's own urgent needs they are not merely uninspiring; they are comforters who bring trouble. It's a magnificent oxymoron, or rather a grievous one. In the English language, "Job's comforters" are people who are trying to be sympathetic or encouraging (or are going through the motions of doing so) but are actually making the situation worse. This is the only passage in Job where the word "comforters" comes, though the verb and noun "comfort" has recurred; the reason his friends showed up was "to comfort him." In the story of Ruth, Boaz provides a neat example of the way "comfort" in the Old Testament can involve both words and actions. Boaz speaks appreciatively to Ruth about the way she has cared for Naomi and prays for **Yahweh** to bless her as she has come to seek refuge under his wings. Boaz has also taken action to ensure that Ruth can glean successfully and safely in his fields. One might see both the actions and words as expressions of the "comfort" she thanks him for.

But Job's friends are comforters who bring trouble. In his first words to Job Eliphaz spoke of the way people who sow trouble reap it, and just now he has spoken of the kind of person who conceives trouble and gives birth to wickedness, though he has not said that Job is such a person. It is Job who takes the initiative in that connection. The well-meaning way the friends treat Job makes the friends themselves the kind of trouble-making people whose terrible fate the friends lament.

To put it another way, their words are tempestuous: they have the destructive force of a strong wind. Job again picks up one of Eliphaz's own expressions, this time from the beginning of his preceding address to Job: "You call my perspective destructive because of the impact it may have on people's faith? I call your words destructive because of the impact they have on me." The word for "tempestuous" is *ruah*, the word that also refers to the spirit of a man or the spirit of God, or to the breath of a man or the breath of God—which can be life-giving or destructive. In his first address, when Eliphaz spoke of the way people who sow trouble also reap it, he went on to see this result as brought about by God's breath, God's angry *ruah*. As Job sees it, then, Eliphaz and the others are as negative in their results as God is when God is bringing disaster on people who deserve it. There's something sick about you, he goes on to say.

If Job were in their position, he could address a sufferer in the way they are addressing him and make the kind of bodily gesture that also signifies sympathy. But the effect of his words would be different. They would actually encourage and strengthen. Once again Job picks up one of Eliphaz's words from his first address, where he spoke of the way Job has fortified suffering people in the past. Neither Eliphaz nor Job tells us what kinds of words fortify, though the continuation of this address by Job and the eventual finale to his story may offer an indication. Job manifests a continuing need to keep talking about the awfulness of his experience, about his longing for God to do something about it, and about how unfair everything is. His friends keep trying to stop him from doing so for his own sake, for God's sake, and for their own sake. At the climax of the story, God does rebuke Job but then tells Eliphaz and his friends that he is angry with them because they had not spoken the truth about God as Job had. At the moment, the friends are sick of Job's going on about his situation, and we as readers may also be tired of it. They and perhaps we have a long way to go if we are to give Job the audience he longs for. The length of the book gives a sense of what it's like to hang in there with a person going through something that is not happening in accordance with our time schedule, something we need God to fortify us for. It can seem too much when we are asked to stay engaged with devastating unfairness and pain for very long.

Here Job goes on to declare that God has worn him out. God has devastated his community (that is, his family). God has shriveled him. People look at him with horror. Whereas he was at peace, God has shattered him (evidently ensuring that people having peaceful lives is not one of God's overriding concerns). They are horrifying things to say about God, but it would be hard for God to deny responsibility for them. Job's other ways of describing his experience, as involving (for instance) people striking him on the cheek or massing together against him, or God piercing his kidneys and pouring his bile on the earth, are metaphorical. They follow the language used in prayer in the Psalms. One significance of speaking this way is to reflect the fact that there is nothing outrageous about Job's words; he is speaking the way one speaks in prayer. The point of prayer is to get God to act, and prayer uses the most powerful and vivid images possible to achieve that end. The images express the real and felt significance of the way God has treated Job. Yes, Job is speaking the truth about God.

In one sense, speaking the truth in this fashion is no use at all. It does not offer relief from the pain or take away the grief, Job points out. Yet Job follows the instinct of sufferers to articulate what they are going through. Something like the lancing of a wound is involved in doing so, even if the wound is going to generate more pus tomorrow. The task of a comforter is to facilitate that process rather than seek to shut it down, as the friends do. Indeed, it is to join with the sufferer in speaking the truth about and to God in this way. One significance of the inclusion of the Psalms in the Old Testament is to enable us to join in prayer with people like Job.

Job has expressed the appropriate response to bereavement in donning sackcloth. Sackcloth is everyday material that only ordinary people would wear, and maybe only at home, so Job's appearing in sackcloth is itself humiliating. It expresses the way his horn (that is, his strength, impressiveness, and status) has been put down. His closing claim takes up the two sides to faithlessness of which Eliphaz spoke. His suffering cannot be explained by there being something wrong with the way he has related to other people or to God.

JOB 16:18–17:16

A Witness in the Heavens?

18 Earth, do not cover my blood;
      there must not be a (resting) place for my cry.
19 Even now, there—my witness is in the heavens;
      my advocate is on high.
20 My friends being people who scorn me,
      before God my eye drops [tears].
21 But he will arbitrate for a man with God
      [like] a human being for his friend.
22 Because a few years will come,
      and I will go the way I shall not return.

17:1 My spirit is broken; my days are extinguished;
      the graveyard is for me.
2 Surely mockeries are with me,
      and on their recalcitrance my eye lodges.
3 Put my pledge by you, will you—
      who is the one who will shake my hand?
4 Because you have closed their mind to understanding,
      therefore you will not be exalted.
5 "For a meal he speaks to friends,
      and his children's eyes fail":
6 He has made me a byword for peoples;
      I have become something at which to spit in the face.
7 My eye is spent through the provocation;
      my limbs are like a shadow, all of them.
8 The upright are devastated at this;
      the innocent person arises against the impious.

⁹ The faithful person holds to his way;
    the man who is pure of hands grows stronger.
¹⁰ Yet all of you, turn back, do come—
    but I will not find an insightful man among you.
¹¹ My days have passed, my plans snap,
    the desires of my heart:
¹² They make night into day;
    light is nearer than darkness.
¹³ If I hope for Sheol as my home,
    lay out my bed in the darkness,
¹⁴ I call out to the Pit, "You are my father";
    to the worm, "My mother," "my sister."
¹⁵ And where then is my hope;
    who can behold my hope?
¹⁶ Will they go down to the poles of Sheol;
    will we descend together to the dirt?

When I was a young assistant pastor in London (what would now be called a youth pastor, but youth pastors hadn't been invented yet), one of the prize members of our largely middle-class youth group was a teenager from the local projects, with which the suburban church otherwise had little contact. He had come to know Christ through the friendship of an older member of the youth group (who himself became an effective pastor in more downtown areas), but he was still capable of getting into trouble with the law, and so once or twice I found myself having to accompany him to court in order to speak with a judge on his behalf to testify to his being a good guy really. I can't remember how effective this was. . . .

Job imagines having someone of this kind to stand alongside him in court. As far as he can tell, the legal system is biased against him, as maybe it was for my friend Mick. He is convinced that, perhaps unlike my friend Mick, he has done nothing very much wrong, at least nothing that makes him deserve the punishment that seems to be exacted of him. He begins by imagining that he is dead and that his death has not come at the end of a normal life span. Soon, he will go to the place from which he will not return.

People in the Old Testament are reasonably accepting of death as the natural end of a happy and complete life, when they die "full" or "full of days" like Abraham and Isaac and David, but Job's reasonable assumption is that he is never going to reach that point (he will turn out to be wrong; that expression "full of days" is used of him at the end of the book). He sees himself as more like Abel, who was murdered. When someone's blood is spilled in that way, although the person can no longer cry out, his or her blood continues to do so. Maybe there is an implication that people cannot rest even when they are dead if their lives have been terminated in that way. But it is not merely the victim who is affected by such an event. A monstrous wrong has been committed, and it should not be ignored, because the world is out of kilter until something is done about that wrong. This would not have to be the execution of the murderer; at least in connection with Cain's killing Abel and David's having Uriah killed, God does not require the execution of Cain or David. But the murder cannot simply be ignored. One might say that Uriah's blood would have cried out from the ground as Abel's did, and that God heard both Uriah's blood and Abel's and confronted David as he confronted Cain, and that even if the result of that confrontation was less than full repentance, it was enough for there to be a sense that the cry had been heard and that the wrong had been acknowledged. Job's desire is that when he is dead, as he expects shortly to be, there will be a sense that the cry of his blood will have been heard and the wrong done to him will have been acknowledged. To that end, the cry of his blood must not be allowed to rest. It must not be silenced.

Yet vindication after his death, when he knows nothing about it, is obviously second best. Job wants to see his vindication. So out of nowhere he comes up with the conviction that there is someone in the heavens, a figure in God's court, who will take up his case even now. The introduction of this idea seems sudden to us, but maybe it would not have seemed so to the audience. The beginning of Job's story introduced the figure of the adversary as if it would be quite familiar to people, and a vision in the book of Zechariah (chapter 3) pictures a heavenly aide of God rebuking the adversary in connection with another "case" that comes before the heavenly court. So maybe Job is appealing to a well-known idea. The heavenly court is modeled on the earthly court (or vice versa). It incorporates figures whose task is

89

to argue for the defense as well as figures whose task is to argue for the prosecution. This person will "arbitrate" for him with God; Job picks up an expression he used at the end of chapter 9. There he declared that there was no one to take up this role. He has apparently changed his mind. There is no indication why this is so; perhaps the only explanation is his desperation.

It is clear that Job has no advocates among his friends; they are simply scorning him. He is thus alone in letting his tears flow before God. This comment points to another responsibility we have as friends when someone we know experiences suffering. It is our job to advocate for them with God. The Psalms likely link with this expectation. The many psalms of protest to God that appear in the Psalter are not there merely for individuals to pray for themselves. They appear there for praying by the family and friends of people who are under attack or who are ill. We forget that praying is the most important thing we can do in a situation that involves injustice. We may rush into situations to "do" something without praying and risk making things worse. Job's friends fail him here, so he is reduced to weeping alone and to relying on the possibility that a figure in heaven will take up his case. His witness or advocate will arbitrate for him or argue on his behalf with God (Job has used this verb to refer to his own "arguing" with God in chapter 13). He will thus act in the way a human being will argue on behalf of a friend in an earthly court.

Job is whistling in the wind. His expressions of hope have a way of yielding immediately to renewed gloom, and so it is here. His spirit is broken. Far from being on the way to fullness of days, his days are as good as extinguished. He is destined for the graveyard. But here, the sense of brokenness returns because he can't get away day or night from awareness of his friends' mockery and "recalcitrance." That last word is an odd one, as it normally applies only to an attitude one takes to people in power, and especially to God. Perhaps Job is now declaring that the way the friends are treating him is an act of resistance to God (a view that God will in due course confirm). He is also again suggesting a link with the Psalms, which provide people such as Job with prayers to pray in relation to the way other people are treating them.

In turn that links with another unexpected move by Job. Instead of dreaming about someone to argue with God on his behalf, he is appealing directly to God, as if the judge is on his side rather than against him. He offers himself as a pledge that he is in the right; he risks forfeiting his life if this is not so. He has no alternative because his friends are against him, so there is no one apart from Job himself to shake hands and thereby commit him or herself to offer surety for him. God has closed their minds, he adds (!), which underlies the mocking way they speak of him as unable to look after his family as a consequence of his sin and the way they abuse him. They offer such a contrast with the stance that upright people would surely take. In contrast to them, Job challenges his friends to come back with a different stance, though he has no expectation that they will do so.

This collection of Job's disjointed words is even harder to understand than some others, and it is hard to find their internal coherence or their coherence with statements he makes elsewhere. Perhaps their incoherence reflects his pain. Further the disjointedness reflects in the poetry the incoherence in his thinking that has been brought about by his experience. This passage also connects with material in the Psalms. Whether he is formally addressing God or not, Job is desperate to get God's attention and to get God to act, and we have noted how the Psalms show that we are free to use any means, to think anything, to say anything, to achieve that end.

JOB 18:1–21

Does Job Dispute the Moral Foundation of the World?

¹ Bildad the Shuhite replied:
² How long will it be until you put an end to words?
    Think, and then we will talk.
³ Why are we regarded as cattle,
    considered defiled in your eyes?
⁴ One who tears himself apart with his anger—
    for your sake will the earth be abandoned,
    will rock be moved from its place?

⁵ Yes, the light of the faithless goes out,
   the flame of his fire does not shine.
⁶ Light darkens in his tent;
   his lamp above him goes out.
⁷ His vigorous steps become short;
   his own plan makes him fall,
⁸ because he is thrown into a net by his feet,
   onto the mesh he walks.
⁹ A clamp seizes him by the heel;
   snares get hold of him.
¹⁰ A rope for him is hidden in the earth,
   a trap for him upon the path.
¹¹ All around, terrors startle him,
   make his feet fly.
¹² His wickedness is hungry;
   disaster is prepared for his stumbling.
¹³ It consumes the limbs of his skin;
   death's firstborn consumes his limbs.
¹⁴ His security departs from his tent;
   he is marched to the king of terrors.
¹⁵ Fire dwells in his tent;
   sulfur scatters over his estate.
¹⁶ Below, his roots dry up;
   above, his foliage withers.
¹⁷ Remembrance of him perishes from the land,
   and he has no name in the outside world.
¹⁸ They thrust him out from light to darkness,
   drive him from the inhabited world.
¹⁹ He has no posterity, no offspring, among his people,
   and no survivor in his place of sojourning.
²⁰ At his fate people in the west are appalled;
   people in the east seize hold of horror.
²¹ Yes, these are the dwellings of the wrongdoer,
   this is the home of the one who did not
      acknowledge God.

Last night we were watching the great movie *Dogma*, which is full of bad language, violence, and scatological humor. It is not a movie for the sensitive or fainthearted or squeamish, but it is one of the most theologically thoughtful and thought-provoking movies of all time. Its premise is that back at the time of the exodus the angel of death and another angel had rebelled against being God's agents of judgment and had therefore been cast out of heaven. They are therefore eternally trapped on earth. But they have now discovered a loophole in Catholic doctrine that will enable them to "go home"; a church in New Jersey is promising forgiveness to anyone who walks through its arch. The problem is that if they succeed in gaining readmission to heaven on that basis, they will destroy the theological and moral fabric of reality by defeating God and getting back into heaven without repenting.

Bildad would totally sympathize with the movie's dilemma. He knows that the idea that wrongdoing receives its reward is integral to an understanding of this being a moral universe. The question is not whether there is the possibility of God's forgiving people for their wrongdoing (which the movie also goes on to portray). God is indeed willing to carry people's sin; they simply need to be willing to own it and accept God's mercy. The question is whether there is any other basis than God's mercy on which people who rebel against God or ignore right and wrong can escape the consequences of their wrongdoing.

As far as Bildad can see, Job rejects such fundamental aspects of a true understanding of God, the world, and humanity and how they interrelate; hence the protest with which Bildad begins. He wants Job to shut up and think through the implications of what he says. When he is prepared to do so, there will be a basis for discussion about the issues his words raise. At the moment there is no such basis. The possibility of dialogue is also imperiled (Bildad says) by the insulting stance Job takes to his friends. Job could be pardoned for seeing this as rather a sassy observation, given the insulting nature of their words to him, but it is often easier to see the shortcomings in other people's attitudes than in our own. As Bildad sees it, Job is treating the friends as though they were no more intelligent than farm animals; maybe this is a reference back to Job's comment about what even animals and birds know (chapter 12). Likewise Bildad's allegation that Job treats the friends as people who are defiled and are therefore to be avoided recalls Job's comment about defilement and the impossibility (humanly speaking) of avoiding it (chapter 14), and suggests that the friends are a bad illustration of that reality.

Job needs to take a look at himself, Bildad suggests. Job is a man consumed by anger; it is as if it is tearing him apart. Bildad is not exaggerating. The issue he raises is, What does Job's anger imply? What does it seek? The teaching of the friends is that God ensures that wrongdoing and right-living get their appropriate rewards, and that what has happened to Job somehow fits that understanding. Job's anger has its basis in the fact that his experience does not match that theory. By implication (Bildad believes) Job is questioning whether there is any moral basis for the way the world works. He is undermining the world's foundations. If Job has his way, he will remove the very underpinning or stability of the world. Bildad knows that there is a relationship between the world's moral order and its natural order, because God is lord of both. Removing the foundation of one imperils the other. It would resemble or threaten emptying the earth of its people or moving the mountains out of their place. Once again, the irony here is that Bildad's declarations are ones that overlap with ones God will eventually make to Job in putting him in his place.

In the meantime, Bildad reasserts the moral nature of the way human life works out. The experience of the faithless is that their lamp goes out—that is, they die. He begins with two lines that picture that reality, then goes back to how it comes about. The man with a spring in his step becomes one who stumbles along, but the second half of the line suggests this may be a metaphor. It describes the way the faithless man thinks things out and makes a decision, and then how his own plans bring about his fall. To put it another way, his own feet make him fall into a trap. Three lines compare him to an animal for which a hunter lays a trap; perhaps there is a link with the earlier comparison with an animal ("it is the faithless person who is as stupid as an animal, not people like us"). The faithless person walks into the trap that he ought to have been able to see, not least because he is used to setting traps. Now, however, he has set one for himself. Terrifying realities startle him and bring about his downfall.

It is not merely that the faithless person brings trouble on himself. It is as if there are forces outside him that bring this trouble on him. It is as if wickedness or trouble is hungry for him, or as if disaster has been prepared for him to make sure that he falls. It eats him up. Bildad continues to personify the forces that take hold of the faithless person, using imagery from Middle Eastern ways of thinking. Death itself is the king of terrors, and Death's firstborn is apparently the son who eats up the faithless and thus brings them to the realm of death.

After death they are forgotten. In our own culture, people often want to leave a legacy. They may like the idea of their names being inscribed on a building. They want to be remembered. The fate of the faithless is to be totally forgotten. No one wants to remember them, at least not in a good way. Likewise, people often want to leave children behind them; it is another form of legacy, another means of being remembered within the family. The faithless will take their children with them. Job could hardly fail to pick up an allusion to the fact that death has already taken his own children. In the immediate aftermath of the fall of the faithless, their fate will arouse horrified reactions all over the world, but they will indeed soon be forgotten.

Yes, that's how the moral foundation of the world works, Bildad affirms again as he closes. When he speaks of the dwellings or the place of the faithless, he may be referring to the homes they have left, whose deterioration he has described, or to the home in **Sheol** to which he has just been alluding. It makes no difference. If you are a wrongdoer, you will meet your reward; wrongdoing refers especially to the way people treat one another, to oppression and injustice. The same is true if you do not acknowledge God. As is often the case, "knowing God" is not merely a matter of having a personal acquaintance with God but also having a practical recognition of God in one's life. It suggests that one recognize that God is God and live in light of that fact. Thus wrongdoing and not acknowledging God again cover the two sides to faithlessness, the way we behave in relation to others and the way we behave in relation to God.

JOB 19:1–29

I Know That My Restorer Lives

¹ Job replied:
² How long will you torment my spirit,
  crush me with words?
³ These ten times you have shamed me;
  you feel no disgrace [that] you ill-treat me.
⁴ Were it indeed the case that I have erred,
  my error lodges with me.
⁵ If you indeed exalt yourselves above me
  and argue about my humiliation with me,
⁶ acknowledge now that God has put me in the wrong,
  has put siege-works around me.
⁷ If I cry out, "Violence," I do not get a reply;
  if I call for help, there is no making of decisions.
⁸ He has barred my way, and I cannot pass,
  and he sets darkness over my paths.
⁹ He has stripped me of my honor,
  removed the crown on my head.
¹⁰ He tears me down all around, and I am gone;
  he uproots my hope like a tree.
¹¹ His anger flares against me;
  he considers me as like his foes to him.
¹² His troops come on together;
  they have built up their path against me;
  they have camped around my tent.
¹³ He has put my kinfolk far from me;
  my acquaintances have certainly become strangers to me.
¹⁴ My relatives and acquaintances have gone away;
  the sojourners in my house have put me out of mind.
¹⁵ My servant girls consider me as a stranger;
  in their eyes I have become a foreigner.
¹⁶ I call to my servant but he does not reply
  when with my own mouth I ask him for grace.
¹⁷ My breath is alien to my wife;
  I am loathsome to my brothers.
¹⁸ Even little children have rejected me;
  when I stand up, they speak against me.
¹⁹ All my close friends detest me,
  and those I have cared about have turned against me.

96

²⁰ My bone sticks to my skin and my flesh,
    and I have escaped by the skin of my teeth.
²¹ Be gracious to me, be gracious to me, you are my friends,
    because God's hand has touched me.
²² Why do you pursue me like God,
    and why are you not full of my flesh?

²³ If only, then, my words were written down,
    if only they were inscribed in a record,
²⁴ with an iron pen and lead,
    engraved on a crag forever.
²⁵ But I know that my restorer lives
    and finally will stand on the dirt.
²⁶ After my skin has thus been stripped,
    away from my flesh I will see God,
²⁷ whom I will see for myself;
    my eyes will have seen him, and not a stranger.
My heart within my breast fails
²⁸ when you say, "How do we pursue him?"—
    the root of the matter lies in me.
²⁹ Be afraid of the sword yourselves,
    because [your] wrath is waywardness [worthy] of
      the sword,
    so that you may acknowledge that there is judgment.

In spring 1741 over a period of twenty-four days, George Frideric Handel set to music a compilation of scriptural texts, mostly from the Old Testament, that had been made by a landowner and patron of the arts called Charles Jennens. In this libretto Jennens was particularly concerned to encourage belief that Jesus was the Messiah predicted by the Old Testament, in a context where deists and Jews did not accept this belief. Whereas Handel's career had been in the doldrums in the 1730s, *Messiah* restored him to public popularity. Part 3 of *Messiah*, which looks forward to the Messiah's second coming, begins with lines from Job 19 (verses 25–27) in the King James Version:

For I know that my redeemer liveth, and that he shall stand
    at the latter day upon the earth:

And though after my skin worms destroy this body, yet in
   my flesh shall I see God;
Whom I shall see for myself, and mine eyes shall behold, and
   not another; though my reins be consumed within me.

Job is not talking about the Messiah, though there is nothing
odd about someone using Job's words to make a different point
from the one Job made. The New Testament does that with the
Old Testament (though it looks as if it had not occurred to the
New Testament writers to take up Job 19 in this way). The Holy
Spirit who inspired the original text can also inspire new uses
of it that have little or nothing to do with its original meaning.
One can see that the words from Job 19, read in the context of
Jesus' death and resurrection rather than in the context of Job's
life, would be a powerful expression of Jesus' significance.

In their context in Job's life, they represent another statement of the conviction that it must be the case that somehow
Job will be vindicated as a man who has lived a life submit-
ted to God, an upright and straight man. That much is clear,
but Job expresses his hope in a tantalizingly oblique way, and
the verses are translated in different ways in different modern
versions of the Bible. Maybe that in itself is a symbol of the
way he is trying to express something that he can only partly
find the words to articulate. It also reminds us that the man
whom the story describes lives with horrible pain and terrifying abandonment. In one sense Job is entirely lucid and is
involved in cool discussion of theology throughout the book,
but maybe the author is more willing than we realize to let Job
and his friends babble on in a more emotional expression than
a merely rational one.

In the Old Testament, a "redeemer" is someone who belongs
to your family but who has more resources or power than you
have and is therefore in a position to help you when you are
in need. One classic situation where the matter arises is where
people are in trouble and are in danger of losing their land or
their freedom. So God can use a person with resources as a
redeemer, though it is possible for this person to forget and
use the resources for self-aggrandizement. Thus Boaz is Ruth's
redeemer, and God is Israel's redeemer, as God treats Israel

as members of his family to whom he has family obligations. A redeemer's task is thus to take your side and take action in order to restore your situation to what it ought to be—hence I use the word "restorer." In this context Job is talking about someone who will restore the situation between him and God. God's hand has touched him in a heavy and negative sense. God pursues or persecutes him (and his friends do the same). And he doesn't know why. So he longs to see God in order that the two of them can sort things out in a meeting of God's assembly of the kind that opened the story. He has to allow for the possibility that in this meeting God will show him where he is in the wrong, but he is really convinced that he will be able to establish there that he is in the right. The role of his restorer will then be to facilitate that meeting and support Job when it happens. The kind of person Job is talking about is the kind of person he described in chapter 16 as his witness or advocate, a person to arbitrate for him with God. (There is thus more than one problem about the idea that Job is talking about someone like the Messiah, and specifically about Jesus. One problem is that Jesus' role was not to establish that we are in the right but to redeem us because we are in the wrong. Another problem is that the idea sets Jesus over against God, as if God is against us and Jesus is for us.)

Job starts the paragraph in question with a desperate plea to his friends that they should have the grace to stop persecuting him; are they still not sated with the way they are consuming his flesh? Eating the pieces of someone is an expression for accusing them, so Job's point may be that they never get enough of doing so to him. The opening part of the chapter gives the most detailed (though doubtless hyperbolic) description of his treatment by them, by the rest of the community, and by God. But in light of the way that this persecution by his friends and by God seems set to continue until he is gone, Job wonders about the possibility of leaving some record of his arguments that will outlast him, inscribed on a rock in the way kings sometimes left a record of their achievements.

If that "if only" can be realized, it will support something that Job is sure about. He has already made clear that he knows that he has a witness or advocate, someone to speak with God on his behalf. How is he sure this is the case? Perhaps he knows that somehow the universe must be a fair place. Or maybe it's common knowledge that there is an assembly in the heavens that decides on issues concerning earth and there are members of this assembly whose task is to make sure that decisions are taken fairly. He knows that there are many divine aides, members of God's cabinet (beings that the New Testament calls angels) involved in the world and aware of what is going on. So he knows that he has a potential restorer there. And while he is not satisfied with the idea that he will find his vindication only after death and not before death, vindication after death will be better than nothing.

As he speaks of his restorer standing "on the dirt" to give his testimony on Job's behalf, it looks as if Job imagines the meeting of the assembly happening on earth. Job himself will be dead and long done; his flesh will have long ago disappeared. He will be in **Sheol**, but the Old Testament occasionally implies that in some sense people in Sheol can be aware of things, so even though Job's body has perished, he may still be able to "see God."

The closing two lines remind us that Job has been speaking to his friends in the context of their relentless persecution and their claim that the root of his problem lies within himself, in his own life or his attitude. Eliphaz earlier spoke of the way the sword threatened the faithless person. Job warns the friends that it threatens them because of their wrath toward him. His conviction expressed in verse 7 is not his final word.

JOB 20:1–29

How Wickedness Gets Its Reward

¹ Zophar the Naamathite replied:
² For this reason my uneases make me respond,
   because of my feelings within me.
³ I hear correction that dishonors me,
   and a spirit from my understanding makes me reply.
⁴ Do you not acknowledge [how it has been] from of old,
   from when humanity was put on the earth,
⁵ that the shout of faithless people is of the briefest,
   the celebration of the impious is for a moment.

⁶ Though his exaltation climbs to the heavens
  and his head touches the clouds,
⁷ like his dung he perishes forever;
  people who saw him say, "Where is he?"
⁸ Like a dream he flies away, and people cannot find him;
  he is driven away like a night vision.
⁹ The eye that looked on him does not do so again;
  his home beholds him no more.
¹⁰ His children seek the favor of poor people;
  his hands return his wealth.
¹¹ His bones were full of his youthfulness,
  but with him it lies down in the dirt.

¹² Though evil is sweet in his mouth
  as he hides it under his tongue,
¹³ as he saves it and does not let it go
  but retains it inside his mouth,
¹⁴ his food in his stomach
  turns into the venom of asps within him.
¹⁵ The wealth he swallows he vomits,
  as God discharges it from his insides.
¹⁶ He sucks the poison of asps;
  the tongue of a viper slays him.
¹⁷ He is not to enjoy the streams,
  the rivers, the brooks of honey and cream.
¹⁸ He returns the gains
  and does not swallow;
  he does not have enjoyment in accordance
  with the wealth of his recompense.
¹⁹ Because he crushed, forsook the poor,
  seized a house that he has not built,

²⁰ because he does not know contentment inside;
  he does not let any of what is desired escape.
²¹ There will be no survivor to eat it;
  therefore his good fortune will not endure.
²² In the fullness of his sufficiency things will become
      straightened for him;
  the full force of trouble will come to him.
²³ May it be for the filling of his belly;
  may he send on him his angry burning,
  and rain upon him with his battle.

101

²⁴ May he flee from an iron weapon;
   may a bronze arrow pass through him.
²⁵ When he pulls it out and it comes out of his body,
   the shining thing out of his gall bladder,
   terrors come upon him,
²⁶ total darkness lies hidden in wait for his treasures.
   Fire will consume him, unfanned;
   may it graze on the survivor in his tent.
²⁷ The heavens will expose his waywardness;
   the earth will arise in connection with him.
²⁸ May a flood remove his household, torrents on the day
   of his anger.
²⁹ This is the faithless person's allotment from God,
   the possession commanded for him by God.

A pastor in the United States has just published a book that begins by questioning whether people who have not believed in Christ will go to hell. The pastor is someone with his finger on the pulse of U.S. culture, and he has been able to build up a huge congregation. The publishers also knew how to work the book's potential, issuing a spoiler video on the Internet a couple of months before the book came out and ensuring that it caused a lot of buzz and a lot of fuss before anyone could actually buy it. So I am among the many people who are writing about the book without having read it, but I am not critiquing the book. I'm simply noting an aspect of its cultural context— which is that hell is not an idea we care much for. Things have changed a lot since Jonathan Edwards's day. A friend of mine is fond of affirming that the reason God punishes people is a desire to purify, which means it's not really punishment but chastisement. The idea of punishment is unfashionable, in general and in religion.

That would be too liberal for Zophar, as it would be for Bildad (and for that matter Eliphaz and Job), whose thesis Zophar again restates. One reason Zophar is troubled by Job's attitude and his questioning is that Job dishonors him by dismissing his teaching. Job is treating Zophar as a fool. But Zophar's talk about uneasy feelings suggests that he is also aware that Job is questioning the foundations of Zophar's worldview. The basis of his attitude to life is that righteousness and waywardness get their reward. If Job is right that this does not work as well as Zophar says, what then is the basis for one's attitude to life? Unwittingly, Zophar is hinting that he himself is vulnerable to the adversary's critique of Job. Is Zophar committed to faithfulness and uprightness only or mainly because they pay (the question that is more fundamental to the book of Job than "Why do the innocent suffer?")? If Job is right, and faithfulness and uprightness do not pay, would Zophar's commitment weaken?

But Zophar does believe that wrongdoing should have its reward, and that it does, and that it has been this way from the beginning. If Zophar had been able to read Genesis, one can imagine that he could have supported his case from there: Adam and Eve, and then Cain, illustrate the point, as does the story of the flood and what happens afterwards. Of course Abel's story is more like Job's, and we don't hear whether Lamech suffered for his waywardness. Wisely, Zophar confines himself to making the point about the faithless. He does not deny that the Abels of this world suffer. He simply affirms that the Cains get their reward.

That is so, he adds, even (perhaps especially) when they are people who do really well and gain significant power. Here his teaching matches that of prophets such as Isaiah, who especially emphasizes that people who are in positions of majesty and prominence get put down. It is true with regard to Israel and also with regard to a superpower leader such as the king of Babylon. Isaiah 14 uses the same words as Zophar in speaking of the Babylonian king's resolve to "climb to the heavens." People who attain a position of power, prominence, or prestige but lack the moral right to be there do not maintain that position, Zophar says. They disappear as quickly as dung that people use for fuel burns up, and they disappear totally. They may look financially unassailable, but their whole financial empire collapses.

Zophar notes that the wayward person takes his family with him. None of them will survive. Isaiah similarly notes that the downfall and death of the Babylonian king will also mean the death of his sons and potential successors. People in a traditional society recognize that they are not merely independent individuals but parts of a family system, bound up together in the web of life. Without belonging to a family they do not really exist in a full sense, and the destiny of the family's head is decisive for the family. The family's life is bound up with that of its head. It benefits from his prosperity and achievements, and it suffers from his downfall.

So the faithless man has to return his ill-gotten wealth, and his children are reduced to begging from the poor. Maybe the implication is that these poor people are ones whom their father had deprived of their land. They now get their property back, and they become people from whom the faithless can and must beg. Zophar refers later to the houses of which the man had defrauded people; he had crushed them and abandoned them to their fate rather than using his resources to sustain them. No matter how much he has possessed, he has never been content; that is how acquisitiveness works. He has never held himself back from fulfilling his desires, and it was inevitably at the expense of other people who ended up as the poor. But as a result he himself is turned rapidly from a man who looked younger than his years (because he could afford to eat well?) to a man who dies before his time.

Zophar has a vivid image for conveying how this comes about. The faithless man is like someone enjoying a good meal, but the food that tastes so fine is the fruit of the wickedness that he so much relishes. There is some inevitability about the way things go wrong and the way such food turns into poison. He has swallowed up people's wealth, but actually it never gets beyond his mouth; he ends up vomiting it. It is a natural process, yet one that God is involved in. God makes him spew it out. To turn the metaphor in a more literal direction, he is indeed in a position to eat well, but he ends up not being able to eat the luxurious food that he can afford. God pours down wrath on him like a warrior raining down attacks in battle. The heavens and the earth have witnessed his faithless deeds, and they proclaim them openly in such a way as to justify and even require this action on God's part. The final irony in Zophar's description of God's action is to call it the giving of an allotment or possession, words the Old Testament elsewhere uses for the gracious, good gifts of God to his people, especially of the land.

Zophar is fine with praying that things may turn out this way for faithless people. He has no particular faithless people in mind, so one significance of such a prayer is that it adds to his own motivation to live a faithful and generous life. (Presumably Job's friends are well-to-do and upright people like Job, but they could be tempted to be led astray by their prosperity and their status.)

JOB 21:1–34

If Only Wickedness Did Get Its Reward!

¹ Job replied:
² Listen properly to my word;
    may this be your comfort.
³ Bear with me while I myself speak,
    and after I have spoken, you may mock.
⁴ Is it the case that I—that my lament is toward a human
       being?
    So why should my temper not be short?
⁵ Look at me and be devastated;
    put your hand on your mouth.
⁶ When I am mindful of it, I am terrified;
    trembling seizes my flesh:
⁷ Why do faithless people live on,
    as they grow older get stronger in resources?
⁸ Their offspring are established before them,
    with them, their descendants are before their eyes.
⁹ Their households are at peace, without fear;
    no club of God is on them.
¹⁰ His bull breeds and does not fail;
    his cow delivers and does not miscarry.
¹¹ They send their little ones out like sheep;
    their children skip about.
¹² They lift [their voice] to tambourine and guitar,
    celebrate to the sound of the pipe.
¹³ They complete their days in good fortune
    and in peace go down to Sheol.
¹⁴ They say to God, "Go away from us,
    we do not want to acknowledge your ways.

¹⁵ What is Shadday that we should serve him,
    and what would we gain if we should pray to him?"
¹⁶ Now. Their good fortune is not in their own power;
    the plans of faithless people are far away from me.

¹⁷ How often does the lamp of faithless people go out
    and the disaster due to them come upon them,
    the destiny he allots in his anger,
¹⁸ [or] are they like straw before the wind,
    like chaff that the tempest snatches away
¹⁹ [or] does God store up his punishment for his children?—
    he should repay it to him so that he acknowledges it.
²⁰ His eyes should see his destruction;
    he should drink Shadday's wrath.
²¹ Because what does he want for his household after him
    when the number of his months has been curtailed?

²² Can one teach God knowledge,
    when he makes decisions over people on high?
²³ One person dies in his full strength,
    all at ease and peaceful.
²⁴ His pails are full of milk,
    and the marrow in his bones is juicy.
²⁵ Another person dies tormented in spirit;
    he has not enjoyed good fortune.
²⁶ Together they lie down in the dirt,
    and worms cover over them.

²⁷ Now. I know your intentions,
    the plans with which you will do violence against me,
²⁸ that you will say, "Where is the leader's house,
    where is the tent that was the dwelling of the faithless
        people?"
²⁹ Have you not asked people who travel,
    not recognized their evidences,
³⁰ that on the day of disaster the evil person finds relief,
    on the day when acts of wrath are carried along?
³¹ Who describes his conduct to his face?—
    he has acted, who repays him?
³² That man is carried along to the graveyard,
    and someone watches over his tomb.

^{33} The clods in the wash are sweet to him;
    behind him everyone follows,
    and there is no numbering those before him.
^{34} So how can you comfort me with triviality?—
    as for your replies, there remains the trespass.

Two or three years before I write, the United States and the Western world as a whole experienced a "great financial meltdown," with a significant factor in the crisis being the way financial institutions lent money for mortgages to people who could not sustain them. Some responsibility for the crisis lay with the financial institutions that introduced irresponsible financial innovations into the process whereby investment worked, and their staff earned huge amounts of money through the fees involved in servicing mortgages. While the national and international issues raised by the meltdown affected and concerned people in general, some of the strongest feelings about the debacle were felt in connection with the senior staff of financial institutions. Virtually none of them were prosecuted, and many of them continued to draw salaries of millions of dollars per year. Meanwhile, many ordinary people lost their homes.

Job is protesting about this kind of reality. He is disgusted with the reality of the way life works out for people who do well because of their faithlessness to God and to other people, and he is hopping mad at God for making things work this way. Eliphaz has accused Job of discouraging people from lament, from the kind of prayer that questions God. You should hear me pray in that way then, says Job.

His experience and maybe the very words of his friends have made him face some realities about how the world works. Facing these realities now scares him, and he does not know where to go with the facts he has now faced. It is easy for someone who is doing well to avoid facing them. Why do faithless people do fine through all their lives and die comfortably in bed? Job does not overgeneralize. He is not denying that some wicked people get their reward or even that most do so, though his question "How often?" comes close to implying that more often than not the wicked continue to do well. He

107

wants his friends at least to acknowledge the fact that some do not get their reward. Conversely, some faithful people do not get their reward, which is the matter that more directly concerns him and is the converse fact that the friends also refuse to acknowledge.

The picture of the good life that faithless people can enjoy naturally fits the social context but is recognizable enough for readers in a Western context. Such people can carry on doing well through their lives, and indeed do better and better as time goes on. They enjoy full and happy family lives with their children, knowing that their children are growing up in a flourishing way and can play safely. They take part in community celebration and festivity.

They have nothing to fear; specifically, no threat from God hangs over them even though they are "practical atheists." It is not that they do not believe in God in theory; it is just that they see no reason to take God into account in their lives. They see no need for prayer, and they hope God will stay well away from them as they stay well away from God. Maybe they never make such a statement in actual words, but the way they live implies it, and it is perhaps what they say inside. And (Job says later) no one dares confront them about their lifestyle. Maybe the systems that put the rich and comfortable in their position stay in place in part because challenging the system would mean the less-well-off will never have the chance to trade places with the rich person. We would perhaps rather have corruption and evil and the chance to become the rich person than have a system that guarantees us only a modest lifestyle. While in theory we would like to be both good and rich, secretly we believe the combination is not really feasible.

Job knows that in reality the faithless are not in control of their good fortune, and he has no intention of imitating their lifestyle. But he can't see why God lets them continue to live in the way that they do. It can even seem that when a day of calamity comes, the faithless do better than the upright. In our own world, fallen leaders commonly leave their countries rich and go live someplace else, a luxury that the poor can't afford. Okay, sometimes the children or the grandchildren see the parents' empire collapse or end up in pain and suffering due to the sins of the parents. This is a form of judgment on the parents, but they never know about it, and Job wants them to experience it themselves. He recognizes in theory that you can't tell God how to run the world, but in practice he is prepared to have a go at offering God some observations. Yes, death comes to faithful and faithless alike. It is the great leveler. In the grave all are equal. Yet the faithless may continue to be honored after they die. They get an honorable burial, and they rest in peace and splendor. The pyramids are a great testimony to this fact.

Job knows that his friends are going to continue reiterating their familiar unrealistic truths as weapons to use against him, for if his friends are right, they will have established that Job cannot be the upright person he claims to be. So his almost-closing statement about the empty triviality of the comfort they offer him is an understatement. More to the point is his actual closing statement, that their replies constitute a trespass, an affront to him. But they are also an affront to God because they are giving a description of God's ways in the world that is simply not true. A statement of the truth has to take into account both the force of what Bildad and his friends say (that God does make the universe work out in a moral way) and also the force in what Job says (that often God does not do so).

JOB 22:1–30

Eliphaz Rewrites Job's Life Rather Than Revise His Own Theology

¹ Eliphaz replied:
² Is a man useful to God,
   that a person of insight should serve him?
³ Is it desirable to Shadday when you are in the right,
   or is there profit when you are upright in your ways?
⁴ Is it because of your submissiveness that he reproves you,
   comes to make a decision with you?
⁵ Is your evildoing not great,
   and is there no end to your acts of waywardness?
⁶ Because you take pledges from your brothers without cause
   and strip the clothes of the naked.

109

⁷ You do not give water to the weary person,
    you hold back bread from the hungry,
⁸ as a strong man to whom land belongs,
    an honored man who lives on it.
⁹ Widows you have sent off empty;
    the strength of orphans is broken.
¹⁰ That's why snares are around you
    and sudden terror frightens you,
¹¹ or darkness you cannot see,
    and a flood of water covers you.

¹² Isn't God high in the heavens?—
    See the loftiness of the stars, how high!
¹³ You have said, "What does God know;
    can he make decisions through the thunder cloud?
¹⁴ The clouds are a screen for him,
    and he cannot see as he goes about the circuit of the
        heavens."
¹⁵ Do you observe the age-old path
    that wayward men have trod,
¹⁶ who were shriveled up when it was not time,
    whose foundation was washed away in a flood,
¹⁷ people who said to God, "Go away from us,"
    and "What will Shadday do for them?"?
¹⁸ But he was the one who filled their houses with good
        things;
    the plans of faithless people are far away from me.
¹⁹ The people who live in the right way see and celebrate,
    the innocent person mocks them:
²⁰ "Is it not the case that those who rose against us have
        disappeared,
    and what was left of them the fire has consumed?"

²¹ Do be useful to him and be at peace;
    by these things good will come to you.
²² Do accept teaching from his mouth
    and lay up his words in your mind.
²³ If you return to Shadday you will be built up,
    when you move wrongdoing far from your tent.
²⁴ You will put precious metal on the dirt,
    Ophir gold in the rock of the wash.

²⁵ The Almighty will be your precious metal,
    your choice silver.
²⁶ When you then delight in Shadday
    and lift your face to God,
²⁷ you will pray to him, and he will listen to you,
    and you will pay your vows.
²⁸ You will make a decree, and it will come about for you,
    and on your paths light will shine.
²⁹ When people make others fall, you will say, "Lift them up,"
    and he will deliver the lowly of eyes.
³⁰ He will rescue one who is not innocent—
    he will find rescue through the cleanness of your hands.

My early years of teaching coincided with a time when many churches were rediscovering the possibility of praying for sick people to be healed and of finding that many were healed. It was an exciting rediscovery, but it raised the question of why some people are healed and others aren't (it was a pressing question for me because my wife had multiple sclerosis, and God never healed her, though we saw God achieve things through her in her illness). You could buy books with lists of the ten reasons why people didn't get healed. When people asked that question, the result was to raise tricky issues for the people praying and/or for the person who was sick. To the burden of being sick was now an added burden. Is my not being healed my own fault? Do I lack sufficient faith, or am I guilty of some sin I haven't confessed?

Job is the victim of a similar instinct on the part of his friends. Someone has said that the friends are prepared to rewrite Job's life rather than revise their theology, and this address by Eliphaz makes that willingness most explicit. Eliphaz begins from the conviction that what we human beings do, whether good or bad, makes no difference to God. God is totally independent of us. By implication, our experience reflects our own actions, not a purpose, desire, or need of God's. Once more the scene in the heavens at the beginning of the story suggests that Eliphaz is wrong, and it opens up for us another positive significance in that troubling scene. Might it be the case that God is remote from the earth and not really

111

involved with us? Might God have started the world off but then left it to its own devices? Is it our job as human beings to get on with living moral lives in the world and seeking for justice there, on the assumption that God may be sitting in the gallery watching what happens below but not actively involved with it? In different ways both that opening scene and the urgent way Job talks to God show that this is not so. Yes, the world matters to God.

If our experience reflects our own actions, what actions might have issued in Job's suffering? His great advantage and disadvantage are his wealth and prominence in the community. He is "a strong man . . . an honored man." Eliphaz knows the dilemmas that accompany privilege. An endless train of widows, orphans, people who have fallen into debt, and people whose families have nothing to eat lines up at Job's tent. He cannot say yes to them all without compromising his own family's future, but that means he has had to say no to many of them. The problem doesn't lie in things he has done but in things he has failed to do. That's what Eliphaz hypothesizes is the basis for Job's experiencing chastisement. It's a frightening hypothesis for people living in the Western world who wonder whether they have any right to be living better than people in the two-thirds world, or for those who know that they are living better than many people in their own country. Maybe that's why we are so unhappy.

As Eliphaz tries to imagine how Job might have sinned (rather a horrible venture of the imagination, when you think about it), there would be another avenue worth exploring. Suppose the problem lies in Job's attitudes as much as in his outward acts? Perhaps he has not publicly worshiped other gods but has secretly sought help from them in the privacy of his heart or of his home. It is a possibility the Prophets sometimes raise. Or maybe he has taken the view that God is not really involved in our lives and has lived as if for practical purposes God does not exist. Strangely, Eliphaz is accusing Job of a stance like the one he himself has taken: God has little reason to care about what human beings do. It also resembles the stance Job attributes to the faithless in the last chapter. In a way, then, Eliphaz is accusing Job of dissimulation in speaking of the attitude of the faithless as if it were not an attitude he himself takes. Job has spoken as if God in the heavens can hardly be aware of all that is happening on earth. This would suit Job fine (Eliphaz implies) because he belongs to the company of faithless people who really want God to keep well away and do not acknowledge that their well-being derives from God, the great giver. It is therefore not surprising that Job is experiencing the downfall such people experience (according to Eliphaz's theology).

But Eliphaz is Job's friend, and he wants to win Job back from his allegedly godless position. Again with some inconsistency Eliphaz urges Job to do something like what he implied was impossible at the beginning of this address, picking up the same unusual verb that he used there. We cannot be of service or benefit to God, he had said. But now he seems to have forgotten this when he urges Job to serve or submit to God. Eliphaz's inconsistency or incoherence in the chapter, like his attempts to invent failures Job must be guilty of, is a sign that he is flailing in his attempt to make theological sense of what has happened to Job. He wants to get Job back to his former position of blessing and to this end wants Job to return to God, but that presupposes that Job had turned away from God. Likewise his promise that God will be the one Job treasures, so he should put aside his wealth (if that is what verse 24 suggests), may imply that Job has been excessively attached to his wealth. In implying this possibility, Eliphaz would be making another guess at the wrong attitude that might have led to such trouble coming to Job.

So Eliphaz promises that Job's relationship with God can be restored. He can enjoy the ideal Old Testament relationship with God that involves lifting his face to God in prayer and praise, having God bless his plans and shine with blessings on his path, and being in a position to show mercy on people who fall and even on the people who cause them to fall. The trouble is that such promises are built on a falsehood: that Job needs to repent of wrongdoing he has not done, like a defendant who plea-bargains by pleading guilty when innocent.

JOB 23:1–17

Who Moved?

¹ Job replied:
² My lament is indeed tormented today,
  though my hand is heavy upon my groaning.
³ If only I knew how I could find him,
  could come to his dwelling.
⁴ I would lay out my case before him,
  fill my mouth with arguments.
⁵ I would get to know the words he would reply to me,
  I would understand what he would say to me.
⁶ Would he contend with me with great strength?—
  no, surely he would set [his mind] on me.
⁷ There an upright man would argue with him,
  and I would escape forever from the one who makes
    decisions about me.
⁸ If I go east, he is not there,
  and west, I do not discern him,
⁹ north where he acts, I do not behold him;
  he may turn south, but I do not see him.
¹⁰ But he knows the way that is mine;
  if he tests me, I will come out as gold.
¹¹ My foot has held onto his path;
  I have kept his way and not swerved.
¹² From the command of his lips I have not deviated;
  I have treasured the words of his mouth more than
    what was decreed regarding me.

¹³ He is one; who can turn him?—
  what he himself desires, he does,
¹⁴ because he can bring to completion what was decreed
    regarding me,
  and there are many things like these in his mind.
¹⁵ Therefore I am terrified of his presence;
  when I consider, I am in dread of him.
¹⁶ God has made my mind faint;
  Shadday has terrified me,
¹⁷ because I am not annihilated in the face of the darkness,
  but the gloom covers my face.

114

A notice that sometimes appears on church bulletin boards says, "If God seems far away, guess who moved?" There's obviously some truth in the point it makes about our relationship with God, but the notice rather tempts me to deface it. I have known times when God seemed far away, and I didn't think I had moved. I recall coming out of a chapel service at my seminary in England and feeling discouraged that I did not feel I had been meeting with God in the way that other people had looked as if they were. I said as much to a student who asked how I had found the service, and he said, "Maybe God wants you to be in that place at the moment." It was a tough response, but maybe he was right, and in due course the feeling passed; I again knew God was present with me. I now talk with people from time to time who don't have the sense of God's presence that they once had, and who feel they are doing all they can to reach out to God but meet with no response.

Job knows that God moved, and he does not know why. We always have to remind ourselves that the Old Testament understanding of God's presence and absence is different from the Western one. We are preoccupied with a *sense* of God's presence. Often, the evidence for us that God is here is that we have a *feeling* that God is here, and the evidence of God's absence is the lack of such a feeling. In the Old Testament the evidence of God's presence is that God does things; God acts in our lives. When Jesus took up the opening words of Psalm 22, "My God, my God, why have you abandoned me," Jesus did not mean that God was far away in heaven. God was present, watching Jesus be crucified, suffering as really as Jesus was, but doing nothing about the fact that Jesus was being executed. God's forsaking Jesus consisted in that refusal to act. It was in that sense that God had moved. Once, God acted in response to Jesus' prayers. Now, God does not do so.

There was a reason for God's abandoning Jesus, and there was a reason for God's abandoning Job. Job has been called a "type" of Christ, and this would link with a sense in which that is so. Job suffered for us, to make it possible for us to face the reality of suffering that we do not understand, to see how to respond to it, and to see how not to try to help someone else who is suffering. Or one could compare Job with the man who was born blind not because of his sin or his parents' sin but because of what God was going to achieve through Jesus' healing of him (John 9). Eliphaz thinks he knows the reason for God's abandoning Job, and Job knows he is wrong. We know the reason; Job does not. All Job knows is that God has withdrawn from him, does nothing to protect him except keep him barely alive (that was the limit God placed on the adversary's activity), and offers no response to his pleas for a meeting at which they can argue about what the hell is going on.

Job begins with a declaration of how tormented he feels and with a comment that implies he is less outspoken in the noise he is making than he might be if he were not restraining himself. His particular reason for wanting to find God is the one that has recurred already in his protests. He wants a face-to-face meeting in order to argue his case with God, to defend his claim to have lived an upright life, and to compel God (!) to tell him why he is suffering in the way that he is. A difference from those earlier protests is that there he had no confidence that he could ever expect to win a case with God, not because his case was not compelling but because God would simply be unwilling to enter into an argument. Here, then, maybe he is whistling in the wind, though perhaps he is able to do so because of the fact that he does speak as an upright man. Maybe he still cannot be sure of the justice of God, but paradoxically he still believes in the justice of reality, of the world. If we abandon that belief, it is hard to stay living, hard to bother with anything. If he still has a hard time believing in the justice of God, then maybe he wonders whether at least the justice of reality will make it possible for him to be vindicated, will compel God to acknowledge his uprightness; and then he will be done with God. He will be able to escape from God, the one who exercises authority over him and makes decisions about him.

The problem is that he indeed does not know where to find God in order to have his confrontational meeting, and after expressing that conviction or hope about what a meeting might lead to, he reverts to the beginning of his present protest. Where does God live? Where can Job beard the lion in his own den? He looks to all four quarters of the compass. The Hebrew

116

expressions are more vivid than the English ones. In Hebrew, people orientate on the east where the sun rises rather than on the north because of the way a compass works. So Job imagines first going "forward," eastward; God is not there. He then imagines going "backward" or "behind" where he is, westward. He speaks of turning to the left—that is, north, if you start by facing east. The reference to the north as the place where God acts may reflect the fact that the north was thought of as the location of God's cabinet meeting, the place where decisions are made concerning events in the world; so it should be a good place to find God, but it wasn't. So finally Job turns right—that is, south, where Mount Sinai was; Israelites were accustomed to thinking of God coming from that direction. That was where Elijah went to look for God when he thought God might be abandoning him to Jezebel, and God appeared to him there. Perhaps God has withdrawn there again? But Job cannot see him. He looks in front and behind, to left and right, and there is nothing.

In speaking of his way and his path, Job reverts to his conviction that he deserves to be vindicated, and that therefore he surely will be vindicated. Job can bring together the expressions "his way" and "my way." They say that "I Did It My Way" is the most recorded song in history, but Job has never sung that song in karaoke in the country of Uz. It's dangerous to claim that I did it God's way, but Job has been driven by his friends to think hard about whether he has done so, and he still makes the claim; we know from the introduction to his story that the claim is justified. Job's talk in terms of testing makes for another ironic link with the events in heaven that set the story going, because testing is exactly what the adversary gets God to agree to. God knew that this testing would prove Job was pure gold. Job also knows that this is so. But he doesn't know that God was convinced about it. Indeed, the idea seems unimaginable because it seems more likely that God needs some serious convincing.

Job claims to have been even more committed to living God's way than God decreed for him, than what God's laws required. His way of making that point is unusual, but the background lies in the way he then reuses the expression "what was decreed regarding me" to refer to the implementing of God's plans in his life, which has been not at all a comfortable business and which may well become even less comfortable. No, God's having a plan for your life may not be encouraging. So when Job thinks about the future, he does so with further apprehension. Yet he has no intention of giving in and pleading guilty when he is not guilty. He is bloody but unbowed. The phrase comes from the poet William Ernest Henry, a TB victim who refused to be beaten by the disease, but it also meant a lot to Nelson Mandela when he was in prison.

JOB 24:1–25

Why Are Times Not Kept by Shadday?

¹ Why are times not kept by Shadday?—
   those who acknowledge him do not see his days.
² People move boundary stones,
   carry off flocks and pasture them,
³ drive away the donkey of the orphan,
   take the widow's bull as a pledge,
⁴ turn the needy off the road:
   the lowly in the land have been hidden away together.
⁵ There: they are wild donkeys in the wilderness,
   who go out in the course of their work,
searching for food;
   the steppe is food for them, for the boys.
⁶ In the open country they harvest their fodder;
   they glean the vineyard of the faithless.
⁷ They sleep naked for lack of clothing;
   there is no covering against the cold.
⁸ They get wet from the mountain rain,
   and for lack of shelter cling to the rock.
⁹ People carry off the orphan from the breast,
   take the baby of a lowly person as a pledge.
¹⁰ They go about naked for lack of clothing,
   and [go about] hungry though they carry sheaves.
¹¹ Between their own terraces they press oil,
   and they tread the winepresses but are thirsty.
¹² From the city men groan;
   the soul of the wounded cries for help,
   but God does not lay a charge of impropriety.

13 Those people—they are among those who are rebels against
        the light;
    they do not recognize its ways;
    they do not live in its paths.
14 At first light the murderer arises
    so that he may kill the lowly and needy,
    and in the evening become like a thief,
15 while the eye of the adulterer waits for twilight,
    saying, "No eye will behold me,"
    and he puts a cover on his face.
16 He breaks into houses in the dark;
    by day they shut themselves in;
    they do not acknowledge the light.
17 Because for them, altogether, morning is deathly shadow,
    when he recognizes the terror of deathly shadow.

18 He is a little thing on the face of the water;
    their allocation in the land is belittled;
    no one turns by way of their vineyards.
19 Both drought and heat snatch away snow water;
    Sheol [snatches away] people who have offended.
20 The womb puts him out of mind;
    the worm finds him sweet.
    No longer is he kept in mind;
    wrongdoing breaks like a tree.
21 He does evil to the barren woman,
    who does not bear a child,
    and he does no good to the widow.
22 Though he dragged bulls with his strength,
    he may stand but not be secure in his life.
23 [God] may give him safety, and he may relax,
    but his eyes are upon their ways.
24 They are on high for a while, then there is nothing of them;
    they are brought low, like a mallow they shrivel,
    like a head of grain they wither.
25 If it is not so, who can prove me a liar,
    make my word into nothing?

Some time ago I used to follow a set of daily scriptural readings
called *Daily Light on the Daily Path* that included verses on different topics for each morning and evening. The verses were

printed on the main body of the page, and the references at the bottom of the page so that you could look them up in the Bible, though the purpose of the readings hardly made it necessary. I was in the hospital once and had lots of spare time, so I started looking up the verses in their context and found to my consternation and puzzlement that many of the encouraging verses about God and God's relationship with us came from the words of Job's friends, whom I knew to be the bad guys in the book. Further, many of Job's own statements were indistinguishable from those of his friends and also indistinguishable from God's own statements when God finally appears to Job. It suggested that the problem with the friends' statements isn't that they are fundamentally untrue but that the friends are absolutizing them. Job, however, reacts in the opposite direction and risks implying that they contain no truth at all.

The last paragraph of this statement by Job (verses 18–25) sounds like the kind of thing the friends would say. It declares that the faithless get their comeuppance. The wrongdoer is like something feeble, flimsy, or lightweight that a current can easily carry away. His land is made likewise feeble and lightweight so that it fails to be productive. There are no grapes to find on his vines, and death takes him away as easily as the summer dries up rivers fed by winter snows. His mother and everyone else forget him; worms eat him; and he resembles a tree blown over by the wind. His ill-treatment of vulnerable women leads to his not being able to maintain the strong position that one would have thought he would occupy. While God lets him enjoy temporary security, God's eyes stay on him. The security fails, and he disappears. The closing words in the last line are then a strong affirmation of the truth of the paragraph, which underlines the striking way in which Job is affirming the convictions the friends usually express. Perhaps he is parroting the friends' words and thus speaking ironically or sarcastically. Or perhaps he is saying he wishes it were so, that God should make it so. I think that it most likely compares with some statements in the Psalms (and earlier in Job) where people declare their confidence about the punishment of the wicked, where the point is that willingness to make such statements is an indication that the speaker does not belong to the company of the wicked. If the likes of Eliphaz are right that Job is a secret wrongdoer and/or is the kind of person who neglects the needy, it would require considerable gall for Job to make the kind of statement about the fate of wrongdoers that he makes here.

This understanding fits with the first part of the chapter, though the opening verse at first seems to clash with it. The context shows that the times and days it refers to are times and days God has set—or ought to have set—for bringing about the punishment of wrongdoers (Job switches between talking in terms of "they" and "he," which Hebrew does more easily than English). God ought to arrange things so that people who acknowledge him and live faithfully see this punishment, but he does not do so. The evidence is the prevalence of the oppressive actions that follow. Moving a boundary stone means robbing a family of its land; Job goes on to refer to the parallel theft of its animals. The result of such actions is to exile the family from the regular life of the community and to turn them into people who have to forage for their food where they can get it. They can no longer fulfill their human vocation of farming their land or look after themselves. On the way to losing their land they lose their children into servitude for their creditors. With further irony, the people whose gleanings they have to be satisfied with are the same faithless people who defrauded and/or hassled them off their land. Moreover, they are involved in harvesting the oil from what were once their own olive trees on their own terraces. Job's description points to the way Middle Eastern peoples commonly turned the slopes of hills to good use by shaping them into terraced slopes on which olive trees, vines, and other fruit trees could grow. Likewise they work as day laborers treading grapes and harvesting grain, but they don't get to drink the juice or the wine or to grind the grain so as to make bread; they go hungry. Having lost their farms, they have also lost their homes, and while sleeping outside may be fine in summer, it's not much fun in winter, and losing their farms also means losing the ability to make proper clothes to keep themselves warm in winter. As regularly happens, it may also make them seek refuge in the city, so that it is from the city that there arises a cry to God for help and for the punishment of their oppressors. But God is like a cop who does nothing to bring charges against such wrongdoers.

The middle paragraph of the chapter goes on from the reference to the city to describe other characteristic problems in a community where social life is breaking down and where there is murder, theft, and adultery. It plays with the twofold significance of light, both literal and metaphorical. Many offenses in these categories are ones that people commit under cover of darkness, which symbolizes the fact that their perpetrators are people who reject the light in a broader sense. Thus the paragraph closes by describing them as afraid of morning because for them it carries the connotations of darkness, in the sense that it is unwelcome.

The first two paragraphs of the chapter, then, have related implications to those of the third. Job laments the way swindlers and other wrongdoers behave in the community, and he laments the way God does nothing about it. While his friends may have driven him into portraying things as darker than they are, he is right that even if we can sometimes see wickedness punished, often we cannot (and thus we long for a day when this happens). It would be hard for Job to lament in this way if he were actually the kind of person Eliphaz suggests he is. His protests about God's lack of action and his statements about the certainty of punishment for wrongdoers have the same implication with regard to Job's own uprightness. His lament thus raises questions about our complicity in wrongdoing. Sometimes we are complicit by making wrongdoing possible, sometimes by declining to take action we could take to stop it.

JOB 25:1–26:14

A Whimper and a Whisper

¹ Bildad the Shuhite replied:
² Rule and awe are with him;
    he brings about peace in his heights.
³ Is there any numbering of his troops,
    or on whom does his light not shine?
⁴ Or how can a mortal be right with God;
    how can someone born of a woman be innocent?

⁵ There: even the moon is not bright,
    and the stars are not innocent in his eyes.
⁶ How much less a mortal, a worm,
    or a human being, a maggot.

²⁶:¹ Job replied:
² How you have helped a person without strength,
    delivered the arm without power.
³ How you have counseled someone without understanding,
    and made known insight in abundance.
⁴ With whom have you addressed words,
    and whose breath issued from you?
⁵ The ghosts are made to writhe beneath the waters
    and those who dwell in them.
⁶ Sheol is naked before him;
    there is no cover for Abaddon.
⁷ The one who stretched out the northern sky over the waste,
    suspended earth over nothingness,
⁸ wrapped the waters in his clouds
    (the thundercloud did not break beneath them),
⁹ enclosed the view of his throne,
    spread his thundercloud over it.
¹⁰ He marked out the horizon on the face of the waters,
    at light's boundary with darkness.
¹¹ The pillars of the heavens quake;
    they are aghast at his rebuke.
¹² By his power he stilled the sea;
    by his insight he crushed Rahab.
¹³ By his wind the heavens were clear;
    his hand pierced the twisting snake.
¹⁴ There, these are the fringes of his ways,
    and what a whisper is the word that we hear of him,
    so who understands the thunder of his mighty acts?

Last night our Bible study group was discussing the story of Elijah's fleeing to Mount Horeb when Jezebel was trying to kill him. There is wind, earthquake, and fire, and also a low whispering sound—the "still, small voice" of the King James Version. What's the relationship among these things? Someone in the group wondered whether God was changing from speaking through earthquake and fire to speaking through a still, small voice, which suits our Western cultural context. We like the idea of God communicating with us through a still, small voice, but in Scripture, there doesn't seem to be a move from one to the other.

Job 26 sees the significance of both whisper and thunder. First, Bildad's final contribution to the debate begins with a description of God's sovereignty. God is the one who is in authority and who therefore draws forth awe, and God does so in the heavens (though no doubt on earth as well). There are both supernatural and earthly forces that resist God; Leviathan and Rahab have already been mentioned as symbols of such resistance. God does not take for granted that even the moon and the stars are all brightness and innocence; they may actually be working against God's purpose. But God has the forces to overcome such powers and can shine his light in such a way as to flush out forces of resistance.

Interwoven with comments about supernatural powers are comments about human beings. The question of whether they are right with God or innocent presumably concerns whether they, too, are truly faithful, truly innocent of resistance to God. Job has argued that he is faithful and innocent and that he wishes he had the chance to face God and get God to recognize it (the continuing irony is that the story began with such an affirmation, but he does not know). Bildad ridicules the idea on the grounds of who God is and of who human beings are. If God is superior to supernatural beings, God must be even more superior to earthly beings like us, beings who are mortal, weak, and on the way to being eaten by worms and maggots. As a man clothed in maggots, Job asked why God thought a mere human being like him important enough to bother with, compared with entities such as the sea or the dragon. Couldn't God ignore any petty rebellions of which Job is guilty (see Job 7)? Bildad throws his words back in his face but gives them a different slant.

Job in turn throws words back at Bildad. Given that Job is a man without strength, whose arm has no power, and who needs deliverance from his terrible predicament, how do Bildad's words help him? Given that Job is a man who does not understand what on earth is happening in his life, has Bildad offered him any actual insight? Who has Bildad consulted in order to get hold of the words he utters? (Answer: no one.) Whose breath or spirit or inspiration was operating through Bildad in giving him his words? (Answer: no one's.) We might hypothesize that Bildad has been keeping company with his own fears and has been saying what he himself needs to hear, to reassure himself that he is not like Job and will not end up like Job. Bildad is talking to himself. And since he is not listening to Job, Job is also talking to himself.

The last paragraph of this Scripture passage at first seems to continue Job's address, but we will see that chapter 27 starts by telling us that Job starts speaking again—which implies that Job is not speaking in 26:5–14. Further, in this part of the book the contributions of the different participants become a bit puzzling (as was already the case in chapter 24). Bildad's few lines were much shorter than anyone's previous addresses, and Zophar never makes another contribution to complete the third sequence in the debate, while sometimes Job says things that would fit at least as well on the lips of Bildad or Zophar (as happened in chapter 24). So scholars have wondered whether the book once contained a complete third sequence of addresses that have gotten mixed up. The trouble is that there is no consensus on how to reallocate the addresses, so I work with the book as we have it. One effect of this arrangement is that the contributions of the three friends peter out; they have said all they can say. I then infer that the new beginning in chapter 27 confirms that the words in 26:5–14 are not Job's words but are instead a statement that is not attributed to anyone. By implication it is a statement by the book's narrator, the person who tells the story (we will see that the same is true of chapter 28).

As such, verses 5–14 comprise another declaration of God's greatness. They begin by adding something to Bildad's words about God's sovereignty in relation to supernatural forces. God is also sovereign with regard to the realm of death. The ghosts (the dead) are pictured as living beneath the earth and below the sea that lies under the earth, which is itself a kind of floating island. **Sheol** and **Abaddon** are two names for that place where the dead live (see the comments on chapter 11). They are exposed to God; death is not a realm where you can escape from God. Thus the dead writhe in fear of confronted by the frightening power of God.

The poem goes on to speak of the heights of the heavens and to describe the process whereby God brought them into being. It was as if God spread a huge tent over the earth. The tent floor is then the earth (suspended over nothingness); the tent is the sky; and the area inside the tent is the space between earth and sky. The specific reference to the north links with the idea that the place where God's cabinet meets is in the north, to which Job maybe alluded in his words about going east and west, north and south. The clouds are the storehouses of the rain, with their capacity to hold the water rather than letting it flood the earth (the same picture as in Genesis 1). They also act as a shield for God's throne in the heavens, to make sure that the dazzling sight of God does not consume people looking up from the earth. It is kind of protective veil.

On the earth, we are surrounded by a circular horizon, which suggests an image for another aspect of God's work. It is as if the horizon sets the limit to the inhabited world that God created and the limit to the realm where light shines; beyond is darkness. Invisible pillars hold up the tent like tent poles (maybe the mountains that rise up to the sky suggest the image of something holding up the sky), but they shake when God acts in power to put down these resistant powers, pictured as the sea or Rahab or the snake.

It's all very impressive. But it's only the fringes of his ways; that is, the impressiveness of the physical world gives you only the slightest impression of God's actual acts and power. Even more significant in the context of the book of Job is that the word or message that we hear is only a whisper of the dimensions of the real truth about God. It is hardly surprising that Job can protest that Bildad offers little insight on how life works and how God works. We only understand the fringes of that. The problem with the friends is that they misconceive the fringe for the whole, the whisper for the full voice. The problem with Job is that he thinks we should be able to understand the full voice. As the debate draws toward its end, the narrator trailers a point that God will elaborate. The book thus gradually starts getting us to think in the way we will need to think in light of the story as a whole. The whisper is important, but we have to remember it is but a whisper.

JOB 27:1–23

I Hate the People Who Hate You

¹ Job again took up his poem:
² By the life of God who has pushed away my case,
    Shadday who has tormented my life,
³ when there is still any breath in me,
    and God's spirit is in my nostrils,
⁴ if my lips speak wrong
    or my tongue utters deceit. . . .
⁵ Far be it from me that I should say you are right;
    until I breathe my last I will not push away my integrity
        from me.
⁶ I hold onto my being in the right and I will not let it go;
    my conscience has not reproached me through my days.

⁷ May my enemy be like the faithless;
    may the person who arises against me be like the wrongdoer.
⁸ Because what is the hope of the impious man when he is
        cut down,
    when God takes away his life?
⁹ Will God listen to his cry
    when trouble comes upon him,
¹⁰ or will he delight himself in Shadday,
    call upon God at any time?
¹¹ I will teach you about the hand of God;
    what is with Shadday I will not hide.
¹² There: you have seen, all of you,
    so why this total triviality you manifest?

¹³ This is the portion of a man who is faithless with God,
    the allocation that ruthless people receive from Shadday.
¹⁴ If his children are many—it is for the sword,
    and his descendants will not be full of bread.
¹⁵ The people who survive him will be buried by Death,
    and their widows will not weep.
¹⁶ If he heaps up silver like dirt
    and lays up clothing like piles of mud,

¹⁷ he may lay up, but a faithful person will wear,
    and an innocent person will share out the silver.
¹⁸ He has built a house like a nest,
    like the bivouac a watchman makes.
¹⁹ He may lie down a rich man but he will not do so again;
    when he opens his eyes, there is none of it.
²⁰ Terrors overtake him like water;
    by night a tempest has snatched him away.
²¹ The east wind lifts him, and he has gone;
    it sweeps him from his place.
²² It hurls at him and does not spare,
    though he flees urgently from its force.
²³ It claps its hands at him
    and whistles at him from his place.

When I have taken part in "quiet days" for reflection and prayer, three favorite Old Testament texts have been the one about the still, small voice that I mentioned in connection with Job 25–26, the "Be still and know that I am God" of Psalm 46, and the reminder in Psalm 139 that wherever we go, God is there. But on other occasions I have been with people who have appreciated Psalm 139 and then discovered that it later talks about hating the people who hate God, and they are disturbed. How can someone who is so spiritually sensitive in the earlier part of the psalm talk about hating in the later part of the psalm?

Some of Job's words raise similar questions, though with a difference. Part of the background is that as Job picks up the microphone again after the narrator has made the comment about our seeing only the edges of God's way, he starts with an assertion concerning his personal integrity. It is a stronger assertion than any he has made so far, though he will make a more detailed one in chapter 31. First, he declares a curse on himself if he is not telling the truth and if he does not do so as long as God's breath remains in him. He asks God to take action against him if this is the case. There is no way he can agree with the aspersions that his friends have cast on his integrity (he uses the same verb to speak of not giving up on his integrity that he used to refer to God's giving up on his case). As usual he is not arguing that he is perfect or sinless but only that he is basically an upright person. He feels that he no more deserves the kind of experience he has had than his friends do, and we know from the narrator's description at the beginning of the story that he is justified in this claim. He could have expressed his point in terms of hatred, like the psalm, a hatred that denotes a commitment to repudiation more than self-righteous indignation or outright prejudice. Hatred of ungodly action and ungodly people (in the sense of repudiation) is a necessary part of integrity. While it may be dangerous to be prepared to "hate" other people whom we see as godless, not being prepared to hate may be more dangerous. Jesus expects people to be prepared to "hate" their parents. Further, being prepared to "hate" and curse oneself may be an indication of being able safely to wield the power to curse—or bless.

Paradoxically, in the same line as he calls down God's curse, Job indicates that God is his problem. God has turned his case aside, which is just the kind of thing you are not supposed to do if you are someone with the authority to make decisions about disputes in the community. God has refused to make a decision for him. That has added to his torment (translations often have the word "bitterness," but Job is not talking about bitter feelings but about the objective bitterness of the fate God has imposed on him). God had begun by tormenting him with the losses described in the opening of the story, but here the observation about tormenting follows the comment on turning his case aside; this is God's second torment of Job.

It is against that background that Job goes on to declare his wish that his enemy or the person who rises against him should have the fate of the faithless person, the wrongdoer, or the impious man. Job has not previously spoken of having an enemy or of someone rising up against him (his "friends" are plural, and for all the force of his argument with them, he does not refer to them as his enemies). He has used another word to refer to a "foe," but this seemed to be a hypothetical person; Job did not have a particular person in mind. Here, too, he is referring to any enemy he might have at some time, and the point of the wish is what it presupposes about the fate of the faithless, the wrongdoer, or the impious because it is what the friends accuse Job of being and what God's treatment of him implies that Job is. In effect he says, "Suppose I have an enemy; then I want him to be treated like a faithless person, a wrongdoer, or an impious man. And you know what that treatment is, don't you?" In case you have forgotten, Job reminds you. He has no hope. He gets cut down by God. God doesn't listen to his prayers. He doesn't get the chance to enjoy a relationship with God. He doesn't get to call on God.

Job is affirming that this is how life works, or at least how it is supposed to work. But the friends view him as an example of a wrongdoer. So if they are right, Job is affirming what should be his own fate. By implication, this is implausible. The irony in Job's address is that he is implicitly declaring that God is treating him as an enemy. Job can't believe that God is doing wrong. He wants God to affirm that Job sees things the right way, but something must be incorrect, or Job's situation would be different.

So, Job goes on to say, I can give you a lecture about how the hand of God operates. In this context, the hand of God is something that comes down heavy on people. It comes down heavy on the wrongdoer, and it has come down heavy on Job, who is not a wrongdoer. The friends know both of these activities of God's hand. Their own teaching emphasizes the first, and they have witnessed the second in Job's life. Of course they think that Job's experience is also an example of the first, but his very willingness to affirm what happens to wrongdoers ought to make them rethink their position. It does not have that effect. Although they have witnessed Job's life, Job's experience, and Job's affirmation, they talk as if they have not done so, as if their old theory works perfectly well. They talk a lot, but their talk is empty triviality. It makes no sense. It does not fit the facts.

In the second half of the chapter, Job goes on to underline what happens to the man who is faithless to God and ruthless in relation to other people. He thus refers to the two aspects of integrity: integrity in relation to God and to other people. His children lose their lives or their livelihood, or they will be buried by death (as it were)—for instance, taken in battle and deprived of proper burial, so that their widows cannot mourn them properly. Their accumulations of wealth and clothes go to others. Their houses turn out to be as flimsy as a bird's nest or a watchman's bivouac. All this may happen with a suddenness that they could never have anticipated.

Job has declared on previous occasions that human life can be this way, but on such occasions he has argued that the process is random and arbitrary. Here his point is a different one. For the sake of argument, at least, he affirms the orthodox teaching that life works out this way for faithless people, for wrongdoers, and for the impious. But his point once more is that if he is prepared to affirm this truth, it is hardly plausible to claim that he belongs to the same category of people. His logic thus parallels that of Psalm 139. Declaring that one repudiates people who repudiate God is not possible if one belongs to the group who repudiates God. The earlier part of the psalm that speaks of it being impossible to go anywhere that God cannot reach fits that fact; it means you are bound to get caught. Job's opening curse on himself if he abandons his claim to integrity would likewise apply to himself if he is actually a wrongdoer. He too would be aware that it is a dangerous curse, because God can indeed reach him anywhere.

JOB 28:1–28

Insight Lies in Submission to the Lord

¹ There is indeed a mine for silver,
 a place for gold that people will refine.
² Iron is taken from the dirt,
 stone that someone pours as copper.
³ He has put an end to darkness,
 and to every limit he was seeking.
Stone in darkness and deathly shadow
⁴ has been broken open by a torrent,
 away from any sojourner.
Forgotten people, away from [human] foot, have dangled,
 away from mortals, and swayed.
⁵ Earth from which food comes forth
 has been changed like fire below.
⁶ Its rocks were the home of sapphire,
 and it had gold dust.

⁷ The bird of prey did not know the path;
 the falcon's eye has not gazed on it.

131

⁸ Majestic beasts have not made a way to it;
    the lion has not advanced on it.
⁹ Someone has set his hand against the flint,
    overturned the mountains by the root.
¹⁰ He has split channels through the rocks
    and his eye has seen every precious thing.
¹¹ He has dammed up the sources of the streams
    so that he might bring hidden things out into the light.

¹² But insight: from where can it be found,
    where is the home of understanding?
¹³ No mortal can know its value,
    and it is not found in the land of the living.
¹⁴ The deep says, "It is not in me";
    the sea says, "It is not with me."
¹⁵ Fine gold cannot be given in its place;
    silver cannot be calculated as its price.
¹⁶ It cannot be weighed out against gold of Ophir,
    against precious onyx or sapphire.
¹⁷ Gold or crystal cannot match it,
    or vessels of fine gold be its exchange.
¹⁸ Coral and jasper cannot be thought of;
    a pouch of wisdom is more than rubies.
¹⁹ Topaz from Sudan cannot match it;
    it cannot be weighed out against pure gold.

²⁰ So insight: from where does it come;
    where is the home of understanding?
²¹ It hides from the eyes of every living thing;
    even from the birds in the heavens it takes cover.
²² Abaddon and Death say,
    "With our ears we have heard report of it."

²³ God understands the way to it;
    he is the one who knows its home.
²⁴ Because he is the one who looks to the ends of the earth,
    sees beneath all the heavens.
²⁵ In setting a weight for the wind
    and establishing the waters by measure,
²⁶ when setting a decree for the rain
    and a way for the bolt of thunder,

²⁷ then he saw it and took account of it,
    established it and also searched it out.
²⁸ And he said to humanity:
    There: submission to the Lord is insight;
    turning from evil is understanding.

In two weeks I have to preach at the seminary's baccalaureate service (a kind of commissioning service, I could call it for U.K. readers). Each year as I have listened appreciatively to the baccalaureate sermon, I have wondered what on earth I would say if I ever had to preach it. Not surprisingly, I did not know the answer when I didn't need it, but when I was asked to preach this year, I knew the answer immediately. I'm not directly preaching on this chapter, but this chapter has the theme. It's easy to think of seminary as concerned with the acquisition of knowledge and skills, but if the seminary gives the impression that these are the only things that people need to acquire, it encourages them to miss the point. The seminary needs to be concerned with insight.

Both Job and his friends need insight. Another word for it is wisdom, the word translations commonly use. It's easy for people to die without ever gaining insight, Eliphaz has declared. Job needs to learn insight from God and from people like Zophar, Zophar has implied. Job has spoken sarcastically about the friends' insight. The book as a whole has implicitly raised the question that recurs in this chapter: where can insight be found? Where can we get some understanding of how life works?

Although this chapter follows on Job's words in previous chapters, its reflective nature stands in contrast to Job's urgency and passion. Further, the next chapter will have a heading that implies Job has *not* been speaking here. So it looks as if chapter 28 complements the last part of chapter 26 in being a reflection that isn't a comment by any of the participants in the debate but a reflection on the part of the person telling the story. Like 26:5–14 it stands back from the debate and implicitly critiques everyone who has been taking part. Chapter 26 noted that we see only the fringes of God's ways. So how can we get that insight?

At the beginning, you wonder how the chapter will relate to the debate at all. What is the point of this fascinating description of the procedures of mining? The chapter recalls the way the Prophets sometimes win their listeners' attention by talking about something that's got nothing to do with what you might think a prophet would talk about (the love song about a vineyard in Isaiah 5 is an example). But it's not simply a homely illustration or a story that wins attention but has little to do with the preacher's eventual point. Ultimately it will relate closely to that point. It anticipates the way Jesus will operate in telling stories that make you listen and then kick you in the teeth. Yes, there are places to find gold, silver, and other precious metals, and miners will go to extraordinary lengths to get access to them. The places are dark, but they bring light to the darkest places. They undertake their risky quarrying far away from where anyone lives and thus in places where no one will think about them. You think about the earth immediately beneath your feet, from which your food grows, but you don't think about workers in the depths of the earth. Agile birds and adventurous animals do not venture where these miners go.

So it is quite possible to find precious metals in the earth, and people put in impressive effort to do so. But what about finding insight? The middle paragraph makes two comparisons and contrasts with the first paragraph. One is that whereas superhuman effort can be rewarded by the discovery of precious metals, superhuman effort does not establish the location of insight. To make things worse, the other is that insight is actually much more valuable than the precious metal in which miners invest so much effort. You can't use it to buy insight.

The third paragraph begins by repeating the question and reprising the point about the inaccessibility of insight. It thus builds suspense. Are we ever going to get an answer to this question, the importance of which the chapter has established? When we are told that God knows the way to it, this comment may not seem encouraging. Indeed, it might seem an obvious fact; the question is whether God is going to keep the information to himself. The paragraph continues to heighten suspense in describing God's sovereignty in relation to insight, and we wonder if we are ever going to get any insight on how to obtain it. Maybe the fringes of God's ways are all we get.

But the chapter again compares with Jesus' parables in turning our thinking upside down with the last line, and it does so in a way that presents us with a decisive challenge. The answer to the question is of quite a different kind than we might have thought. The key to acquiring insight isn't huge physical or intellectual effort. Lo and behold, it is the qualities that the beginning of the story told us that Job has: submission to God and turning from evil (see the comments on 1:13–22). The implication is that Job is a man of insight! Does this imply that Job's repeated questions and challenges are expressions of insight, not of foolishness or ignorance (as the friends have implied)? Or does it rather suggest the opposite, that Job has the insight that counts but that the insight that counts is not the one that has the answers to all the questions that Job's experience raises? Either way, in a fashion typical of the way the story works, the chapter trailers a theme that will be more explicit later. If God rebukes Job for his questioning, God also comments on the fact that he has been telling the truth in a way that the friends have not.

The poem is not addressed to anyone within the book; like the main story it is addressed to the people who read the book. Its challenge thus addresses them (that is, us) and declares that if they (we) are people who want to gain insight, what is needed is submission to God and departure from evil. Many people come to study Job because they think they may find there the answer to the problem of suffering, but it transpires that the "answer" the story offers is of a different kind from the one we thought. Many people come to seminary because they think they may find there answers to theological questions that have puzzled them and that discovering these answers will sort them out. In the seminary they can get a degree and thus a document that is implicitly a certificate declaring that they have insight. They get this document without anyone asking questions concerning their piety or morality, their submission to God or their rejection of evil. It looks as if seminary certificates are therefore spurious. People may have collected information by means of their program, but it is not an indication that they have acquired insight.

JOB 29:1–25

The Way We Were and the Way I Thought We Would Be

¹ Job again took up his poem:
² If only it was like gone by,
   like the months gone by when God was watching over me,
³ when his lamp was shining over my head,
      when I was walking through the darkness according
         to his light,
⁴ as I was in the days of my harvest time,
      when God's council was over my tent,
⁵ when Shadday was still with me,
      my young people were around me,
⁶ when my feet bathed in cream,
      and the rock poured streams of oil for me,
⁷ when I went out to the gate of the town,
      set up my seat in the square.
⁸ Boys saw me and withdrew;
      old men got up, stood.
⁹ Leaders held back words,
      put their hand to their mouth.
¹⁰ The voices of rulers were quiet;
      their tongue stuck to their palate.
¹¹ When the ear heard, it wished me good fortune;
      when the eye saw, it testified to me,
¹² because I rescued the afflicted person who cried for help,
      the orphan who had no one to help.
¹³ The blessing of the person who was perishing would come
         upon me;
      I made the heart of the widow shout out.
¹⁴ I put on faithfulness so that it clothed me;
      my making of decisions was robe and turban.
¹⁵ I was eyes to the blind person;
      I was feet to the lame.
¹⁶ I was a father to the needy;
      I sought out the case of the person I did not know.
¹⁷ I broke the jaws of the wrongdoer
      and took the prey out of his teeth.

¹⁸ I said, "I shall breathe my last with my nest;
      I shall make my days as many as the sand,

¹⁹ my root open to the water,
    dew lodging on my branches,
²⁰ my honor fresh with me,
    my bow renewing itself in my hand."

²¹ People would have listened to me and waited;
    they would keep quiet for my counsel.
²² After my word they would not speak again;
    upon them my word would drop,
²³ and they would wait for me as for rain;
    they would have opened their mouth as for the late rain.
²⁴ When I would smile at them, they would not believe it;
    the light of my face they would not discount.
²⁵ I would choose the way for them and preside as head
        for them;
    I would dwell like a king among his troops,
    like one who comforts mourners.

They say that if your spouse dies after a time of illness and/or gradual decline, initially your memories are dominated by the nature of those last months, but that eventually older memories come to reassert themselves, memories of the time when the person you loved was well and flourishing and your marriage was more joyful. When my first wife died after being ill for many years, I doubted whether this would be the case because it was nearly thirty years since she had been really well. I tried to encourage the process by putting up photographs dating from the earlier years of our marriage, yet even this action generated mixed feelings. The person she was thirty years ago was so different from the person she became that looking at the photos simply heightened a sense of resentment and/or sadness about the way her illness affected her.

Job has some overlapping feelings. His memories are poignant and painful. His starting point is his profoundly painful recollection of God's watching over him. (He has spoken more than once about God's continuing to watch over him, but now God does so in a negative way, as if watching out for his mistakes and for ways to chastise him.) Even without the help of photographs he can remember when God's watching was more like God's watching over Jacob when he fled from Esau, the watching to which Aaron's blessing refers, or the watching promised in Psalm 91 or Psalm 121. He can remember it, but his more recent experience has been that negative watching. The old watching expressed itself in God's light shining (Aaron's blessing speaks of that experience, too), giving him life and also enabling him to see where he was going. Now he does not know the blessing that light suggests, nor does he know where he is going.

In English, speaking of the autumn of my life would suggest my life was coming to its end, but for a Middle Eastern person, harvest time is the time of fulfillment and achievement, when the crops come to fruition. Job was in the prime of life, we might say. To say that God's council was over his tent may imply that this council (the heavenly cabinet) was also watching over him, or that the deliberations and decisions of such a body and of God in person were with Job, giving him enlightenment (we might then use the word *counsel* rather than *council*). Either way, there is another ironic link and point of tension with the account of God's assembly that opened the story, which Job does not know about.

God's being with Job is another way of referring to God's active presence and blessing. It had once issued in Job's being surrounded by his "young people," his children whom we know from the beginning of the story to be young adults. But when God withdrew, the young people lost their lives. It's said to be one of the toughest human experiences when parents have to bury their children instead of the other way around, and Job has had to do so. Once, his family's farm had so many sheep and olive trees that it was as though milk and olive oil flowed in rivers down the street, and you could bathe in it. But that's all past.

Job spends more time recalling his respected place in the community. He would regularly join other leading men in the square at the town gate where they dealt with community business and no doubt shared gossip. There he would naturally be respected not only by the younger members of the community but also by his peers and elders. They would hold back from expressing an opinion until they heard what the wise Job would say.

Why was Job held in such respect? The second part of his recollection explains. People wished him good fortune and testified to his character on the basis of hearing what he said and seeing what he did. One of the tasks of the community leaders was to sort out matters of conflict in the community and see that the needy were treated properly and fairly. It's clear from the Prophets that in practice, in keeping with usual human custom, the people in power used the procedures of such a gathering to further their own interests. Job can claim to have resisted this temptation; he would therefore be able to use his influence to see that the assembly also did not do so. He could thus protect the afflicted, the people without power in the community, people who would otherwise perish. Among them would be the orphans and the widows, people who had no man to protect them and take their side. In their vulnerability, they would easily be the needy, the people with no one to provide for them. There would also be the blind and lame, of whom it is easy to take advantage, as well as strangers in the town, the people who had never had family there and whom no one knew, and whom Job did not know.

When Job speaks of breaking people's jaws, maybe he speaks metaphorically; literally, it was through his contributions to the work of the assembly that he took action. But the words imply a recognition that the assembly needed to use force where necessary, and Job was prepared to do so. It is all part of being a person characterized by faithfulness in the making of decisions (righteousness and justice, in traditional translations). Neither God nor human bodies can see to social justice unless they are prepared to be violent or to be associated with violence, and Job was so prepared.

Job had a position of honor because of his stance, and he naively expected that it would continue into the actual autumn of his years. There he was, cozy in his nest, and he thought he would end a long life there in peace, well-sustained and prepared until the end to wield his bow—again, literally or metaphorically. He would keep his honor, and people would continue to pay attention to his opinions. When he expressed appreciation of them, their words, or their actions, they wouldn't be able to believe their luck. They would certainly not discount it (literally, they would not let it fall)—in fact, they would do the opposite. Indeed, he would be like a chief or a king in the assembly. In principle Israel did not believe in having people like mayors,

139

senior pastors, governors, and judges. Rather than individuals holding such positions, they believed in corporate leadership. But Job's informal authority, which arose from his integrity and submission to God and the fruits of that commitment that were evident in his life, would be such that he would be in a key leadership position. He would even be the person who comforted the community in time of disaster. But he has turned out to be someone mourning, with no comforter.

JOB 30:1–31

The Way We Are

1 But now people mock me,
   people younger than me in days,
 people whose fathers I would have declined
   to put with my sheep dogs.
2 Indeed, what use would the strength of their hands be to me,
   when their vigor has perished from them,
3 people who because of want and desolate hunger
   flee to the arid regions in the evening, to the devastating
      devastation,
4 who pick the saltwort on bushes;
   the root of broom is their food.
5 They are driven out from society
   (people shout at them like a thief),
6 to dwell in the gullies of washes,
   holes in the ground and rocks.
7 They bray among the bushes,
   huddle under the thistles,
8 children of rogues, yes, children of people with no name,
   they are struck down from the land.

9 And now I have become their song;
   I have become a byword for them.
10 People abhor me; they stay away from me,
   but they do not hold back spit from my face.
11 Because someone has loosened my bow and humbled me,
   they have thrown off restraint in my presence.
12 When a brood arises at the right,
   they make my feet fall,

and they build up roads against me to bring disaster.
¹³ They break down my path;
    they promote my destruction;
    there is no helper in regard to them.
¹⁴ They come through a wide breach,
    come rolling through the devastation.
¹⁵ Terrors are turned upon me;
    like the wind it chases off my honor;
    my deliverance passes away like a cloud.
¹⁶ So now my life pours out from me;
    days of affliction take hold of me.
¹⁷ Night pierces my bones,
    and the people who gnaw at me do not rest.
¹⁸ With great force one grasps [me like] my clothing,
    girds me like the neck of my garment.
¹⁹ He has thrown me into the mud,
    and I have become like dirt and ashes.
²⁰ I cry for help to you, but you do not answer;
    I have stood up, and you have looked at me.
²¹ You turn into someone cruel to me;
    with the power of your hand you are hostile to me.
²² You lift me to the wind, make me ride on it,
    and dissolve me with a crash,
²³ because I know you will turn me to death,
    to the meeting house for every living person.

²⁴ Surely someone does not stretch out a hand at a wreck,
    if in calamity there is a cry for help to them.
²⁵ Did I not weep for one whose day was hard?—
    my heart grieved for the needy.
²⁶ Because I looked forward to good fortune,
    but evil came; I hoped for light, but darkness came.
²⁷ My insides churn and do not stop;
    days of my suffering confront me.
²⁸ I walk about dark, without warmth;
    I arise in the assembly and cry for help.
²⁹ I have become a brother to jackals,
    a companion to ostriches.
³⁰ My skin turns black on me;
    my bones burn with heat.
³¹ My guitar has become for mourning;
    my pipe for the sound of weepers.

Today a woman came to see me and wept. Her husband left her after ten years of marriage, leaving her with two small children to look after. On her account, his leaving came right out of the blue; there was no clue that he was unhappy in the marriage. But since he left and went to live with another woman, she has worked out that he actually had more than one affair. They were the joint pastors of a local church, and she has had to face the fact that they have been living a lie in their relationship with the church, where she sought to serve God with her husband for those ten years. The church has grown, and she imagined they would stay there for quite a long time and see more growth. Her husband had talked about their growing old together. Now many people in the church are taking her husband's side. The past has lost its meaning. She is not clear what, if anything, she can hope for from God for the future.

It's an experience more women live through than men do. In a traditional society, at least, men are more likely to tell a story like Job's, in which their sense of loss relates to losing their position in the society. Indeed, Job's starting point lies in people's mockery. One of the problems with mockery is that it buttresses buried fears we may already have. I doubt whether I count, one thinks, whether I matter, whether I have any significance. "No, you don't," the mockery says (if we do not have such fears, the mockery will likely be something we can laugh off).

Today as my wife and I walked down the main street of our city through the Saturday crowds, a homeless person asked for some change. In Job's case the homeless beggars had reason to mock him rather than ask for help, which is an indication of how deeply he is in trouble. The irony about the mockery is that it comes from people who have not been able to maintain their own positions in the community. They have been forced to take refuge outside the ordered setting of the town and its environs and to find shelter and forage for food in the wilderness, where nothing very edible grows. Unlike many of the homeless in our society, they are not people who are the victims of unfortunate events or societal neglect but "the children of rogues"—such expressions in Hebrew imply that they are rogues themselves. They are people you wouldn't trust your sheep to, and you would keep your eye on your purse when they were around. It is such people who sing taunting songs and tell mocking stories about Job—in his imagination, at least.

The content of the taunts in the middle paragraph of the chapter may be that of the mocking by these social outcasts, though its content perhaps suggests taunting by people in general. In any case, we again should not interpret Job's words literally. They constitute another expression of how he feels and of the implications of people's attitudes, and like such statements in the Psalms, they are not necessarily a guide to what people actually did. That fact is hinted in the line declaring that people both keep away from Job and spit in his face (the same people cannot do both, at least not at the same time). Loosening the bow means disabling his weapon. Job is disarmed and put down, and people have no need to hold themselves back in attacking him. On one side a group assaults him with the intention of making him collapse, assailing him like a besieging army building up siege ramps in order to conquer a city. They block off his way of escape, as it were, in order to make sure he gets destroyed. He has no help, and eventually they breach the city and march in. Terrifying forces overwhelm him and quash the honor in which he is held; any possibility of rescue vanishes. Put more literally but still poetically, he can sense his life ebbing away. By day and by night affliction attacks him. It's as if people are gnawing away at him, or as if one of them grabs him as tight as his own clothing does and knocks him down into the mud so that he is covered in dirt. The description is vastly overstated, but the fact that you are paranoid doesn't mean people aren't against you. And words can have a devastating effect. That's why we pretend that sticks and stones can break our bones but being called names doesn't hurt us.

In the Psalms, people's prayers commonly speak in terms of how *other people* are acting, of what *I myself* am experiencing, and of what *you* God are doing or not doing. The third paragraph comes to the third way of speaking. You, God, says Job, do not respond to my plea for help. You look at me when I stand, in the posture of someone appealing to a superior authority, but looking is all you do. Instead of responding to me, as people in authority should, you behave like the ruthless authorities whom the prophets critique. You lift me up so that the wind can carry me away like chaff, which is what God is supposed to do to the wicked but not to someone like me. I know you are taking me to death, to the place where all humanity is eventually due to meet. And that means you are behaving in less than human fashion. Even a human being does not lay a hand on a person who is already a wreck, especially if that person is crying out for help in the midst of calamity. Yet that is what you are doing. And there is no basis for that action in the way I have behaved toward the needy and toward people who are having a hard time. In other words, instead of your telling me to be like you, I bid you to be like me.

How brave Job is in his daring confrontation of God and in how far he will venture to provoke a response from God, somehow, anyhow. It would be better to get struck dead for blasphemy than to continue to be ignored. His last five lines again remind God and us of how desperate he feels. He is hopeless, gloomy, churning inside, dark, cold, disregarded, burning hot (again the contradiction warns against our taking him literally). Like the exiles in Babylon in Psalm 137 who had hung up their musical instruments because there was no way they could sing praise psalms, Job cannot make music that is joyful, only that which is doleful. If you are a musician, not being able to make music has a particular pain.

JOB 31:1–12

The Way I Have Walked (I)

¹ I have sealed a covenant for my eyes,
   so how could I think about a girl?
² What is the allocation that God gives from above,
   the lot that Shadday gives from the heights?
³ Is disaster not for the wrongdoer,
   ruin for the people who act wickedly?
⁴ Does he not see my ways,
   take account of all my steps?

⁵ Have I walked with emptiness;
   has my foot hastened after deceit?

144

⁶ He should weigh me on faithful scales,
   so that God may acknowledge my integrity.
⁷ If my step deviates from the way,
   or my mind has gone after my eyes, or a stain has stuck
      to my hands,
⁸ may I sow, but another eat;
   may my crops be uprooted.

⁹ If my mind has been enticed by a woman,
   or I have laid in wait at my neighbor's door,
¹⁰ may my wife grind for another,
   and over her may other men kneel,
¹¹ because this would have been deliberate wickedness;
   it is waywardness for the mediators [to deal with],
¹² because it is a fire that consumes to Abaddon,
   and it would uproot my harvest.

A year after my first wife Ann died, I was out to dinner with a group that included a former colleague whose wife had died a while previously. He had remarried a year or so later, and I was intrigued to hear the story. He began from the aftermath of his wife's death, when another colleague who is a professor of pastoral counseling had told him, "Don't marry someone young enough to be your granddaughter." The story made us laugh, but it was sage advice, in that one sees pictures from time to time of eighty-year-old men who have married twenty-five-year-old women, and one wonders how they overcome the disparity in life experience and expectations. (If you are part of a happily married couple with such an age difference, congratulations; there are exceptions to every rule).

It's therefore striking that Job's account of the integrity of his life begins with his abhorrence for the idea of thinking about a girl. The word for a girl suggests a teenager, someone young enough to be unmarried. Job is married, but a man of his prestige in the community might be expected to have more than one wife. The stories of David and Solomon illustrate how traditional societies often assume it is appropriate for an important man to have several wives (even though the Old Testament also implies a question mark about whether things should really be this way). So there might be nothing illicit about Job's fancying a young girl, whom he might marry, and his commitment to avoid doing so implies a commitment to noteworthy sexual fastidiousness. Job is a man, and it looks as if Job knows that men think about sex a lot. So sex is the concrete starting point for understanding "wrongdoing" and "wickedness" and for a recognition that without a commitment to sexual propriety, he is liable to God's bringing disaster on his life. That disaster will be his "allocation" or "lot" from God. It is clear enough in any age that sexual indulgence is an easy way to bring disaster on one's life. While Christians can be too preoccupied with sexual sin, sex is such a powerful force and such a problem for men that there is also danger in underestimating the importance of sexual sin.

Literally, Job speaks of "cutting" a **covenant** for his eyes. The expression apparently refers to a ceremony that could be involved in making a covenant. You could cut an animal in two and pray that the same fate would overcome you if you fail to keep your covenant. Further, Job speaks of making a covenant *for* his eyes. When you make a covenant *with* someone, the expression implies a mutual agreement and commitment. When you make a covenant *for* someone, the expression implies a more one-sided action. The party making the covenant is not asking for the other party's opinion but simply saying either "I am making this commitment to you whether you like it or not" or "I am expecting this commitment from you whether you like it or not." So here Job is imposing a covenant on his eyes—obviously it is a covenant he will be involved in keeping. Imposing it on his eyes recognizes that men are characteristically more visual than women in their sexual instincts. It's therefore a help to men when women dress modestly—the problem belongs to the men, not to the women. Further, a man's giving freedom to his eyes encourages him on the path toward thinking about sex and toward physical indulgence.

Reference to the eyes recurs in the middle paragraph, when Job moves to comment on what we might think of as more social sin. He speaks first of having nothing to do with emptiness; characteristically, the second half of this line clarifies what he means when it goes on to speak of deceit. "Emptiness" connotes something with no reality behind it. Job is referring to his society's equivalent to scams and rip-offs, confidence tricks and Ponzi schemes. The stimulus to such deceit is covetousness; hence the significance of the Ten Commandments' ending with covetousness, and the danger of the fact that Western economies are based on covetousness. The danger is that our mind goes after our eyes—our thinking and our plans come to focus on how we can acquire what we see. In turn our steps follow where our minds have gone and ignore the way God and morality prescribe. The acquiring naturally also requires hands that do the taking or receiving, and if the acquiring has involved dishonesty, then these hands acquire stain. Job's words bring together one's eyes, mind, hands, and feet; "integrity" and "faithfulness" involve the whole person. As you are affected by pollution if you have been in contact with death and you have to seek cleansing before you come into God's presence, so you are affected by pollution if you have been in contact with things that are morally incompatible with God's own nature. You can't go into God's presence if you are affected by such pollution, or if you do so without first seeking cleansing, you risk trouble for yourself and your community. Job assumes that the deceit he speaks of would undermine even someone's basic need to grow one's food, let alone success in getting one's most far-reaching desires fulfilled. The internal interdependence of the elements of the created world means you can expect nature itself to become involved in ensuring this result, and Job is sufficiently confident of his integrity to declare the hope that he will fail here if he has indeed been involved in deceit.

In the third paragraph he returns to sex, confirming that it is a major male preoccupation. Whether or not there is anything inherently wrong about fancying a young girl, there is no doubt when it is a question of fancying the woman next door. It is a vivid picture, the image of a man like Job hanging around his neighbor's house hoping to get another look at the woman of the house, or maybe hoping for more than a look. We talk as if we are simply overcome by love, but it requires our cooperation. Adultery demands planning. It is a deliberate action.

One might, however, commit adultery for reasons beyond sex. In our culture, the obvious reason is that a man gets bored with his wife or fed up with aspects of who she is and what she does. Presumably that could happen to men in Job's culture. But when the tenth commandment warns about coveting the woman next door, it sets her alongside houses, servants, and animals, which might suggest the coveting has a more practical concern. Maybe the woman next door is closer to realizing the ideal of Proverbs 31. In the ideal household as the Old Testament understands it, a husband and wife are partners in the family business, and a man could easily be jealous of his neighbor's having a partner who holds up her end of the household's responsibilities better than his wife does. David's story implies that the reason he wanted Michal (before and after she was someone else's wife) and wanted Abigail wasn't sexual; it was practical.

Again Job is prepared, even enthusiastic, for the punishment to fit the crime. Crime indeed it is, as the reference to the mediators suggests. Adultery between two consenting people is not just their private business. The harmonious life and functioning of the village is imperiled by adulterous relationships, as by other causes of conflict. It is not just a matter of families not speaking to one another or of private fights between a couple of men or a couple of women. Adultery would threaten breakdown in the society; it could terminate the cooperation on which the very life of the village depends. That is why the resolution of the issues it raises involves the community's "mediators," the people anyone can appeal to when a dispute needs resolution. They will be the elders with whom authority lies in the community.

Job sees that it would be appropriate for his adultery to issue in his own wife's becoming the sexual partner or victim of other men, with the shame that would bring to him. (If it seems that Job is being callous in his attitude to his wife, then we need to recall that he is talking only in theory, given that the point of his words is to underline the fact that he has *not* put his wife in this danger.) In Western culture, as in a traditional society, we know how calamity often follows adultery. No divine intervention is required, but it may be hellish in its effect.

JOB 31:13–23

The Way I Have Walked (II)

¹³ If I have rejected the case of my male or female servant
   when they contended with me,
¹⁴ what will I do when God arises;
   when he pays attention, what will I reply?
¹⁵ Did not my maker make him inside his mother;
   did not one person form us in the womb?

¹⁶ Do I hold back from the want of poor people,
   or make a widow's eyes fail,
¹⁷ and eat my meal alone,
   so that the orphan has not eaten of it?
¹⁸ Because from my youth he has grown up with me like
      a father,
   and from my mother's womb I have guided [the widow].
¹⁹ If I see someone perishing for lack of clothing,
   and a needy person has no covering,
²⁰ if his heart has not blessed me
   when he gets warm with the shearing of my sheep,
²¹ if I have shaken my hand against the orphan
   because I could see that I had help at the gate,
²² my arm should drop from the shoulder,
   my forearm break from the socket,
²³ because I would have had fear of disaster from God,
   and I would not have been able to bear his majesty.

On Sunday we had a meeting to discuss our church's ministry to homeless people; many live in our area, and we are next door to a community center. They know that Sunday morning is an obvious time to drop by to see if we have food, and we try to keep food supplies on hand to give to them. One topic of our conversation, however, was that their instinct is to look for the rector and the instinct of members of the congregation is to refer them to the rector, which is a problem not least because he needs to be getting ready for the services. Yet there is something right about that instinct. There is a sense in which the rector is the head of a household, of the church congregation, and one of the commitments of the head of a household is to see that the household's resources are made available to people in need.

Job understood this commitment, and he could claim that he had fulfilled his responsibility as head of the household or head of the family. Admittedly both household and family are tricky words, because in a traditional society they mean something much bigger than a household or family in the Western world. In Israel, the average village might comprise up to two hundred people, and they might belong to about three families, which would then comprise a number of households. The family and the household incorporate three or four generations of people who are directly related to one another—parents, their grown-up children, their children, and maybe an older generation of aged grandparents. But they also incorporate people from other families, such as widows and orphans, male and female servants, and resident aliens, people whose own relatives no longer survive or who have had to separate from them for some reason. In such a society the idea of an individual living alone does not exist as a proper or practical notion, and the family is the society's structure for ensuring that no one needs to try to do so. The family is society's safety net, and it is large enough to have the potential not to be too oppressive. The family as a whole comprises enough households to allow you to take refuge in another to avoid tension or abuse in your own.

Such is the theory, though the Old Testament makes clear that things don't always work out in accordance with the theory. Families are affected by the human selfishness that they are also designed to counteract and compensate for. Job's claim is that he has fulfilled the obligations imposed on him as the head of the family. It is his job to see that disputes and conflicts in the family are resolved rather than brushed under the carpet and to do so in a way that concerns itself with the needs of the people who have no power (another irony: within the family Job has served as a mediator and advocate for the powerless, but he is now in need of a mediator himself). One can imagine that the people who belong to the family by birth and have a guaranteed permanent place in its future would be tempted to ill-treat the people who are there as servants. Some translations refer to them as "slaves," but we noted in connection with

150

chapter 7 that this word is misleading. Obviously people who were "slaves" in the sense with which we are familiar in the Western world would not be people who expected to be able to complain to their master. One can imagine that some of these servants might be lifelong family servants like Abraham's servant in Genesis 24. Others might be short-term servants like those envisaged by the regulations in the **Torah** and elsewhere in the Middle East concerning indentured servitude for debt.

The existence of these regulations presupposes that servants were liable to unfair treatment, and one can imagine disputes arising between servants and other members of the household, including Job. Either way, as the head of the household he is responsible for whatever happens. Moreover, he assumes that members of his household staff can approach him directly, and he claims that they would get fair treatment. The language he uses in verse 13 ("the case," "they contended") belongs in the context of formal dispute procedure—it is the language he uses for the case between him and God and for the way he contends with God. Perhaps he recognizes that his claim to be able to contend with God and to bring his case to God implies that his servants have the right to contend with him and to bring their cases against him. Or perhaps he feels that if his servants can act in this way, God should likewise recognize that Job can act in this way in contending and bringing a case.

More explicitly, Job makes two related points. One is that he recognizes that God is his servants' protector, so Job has a pragmatic reason for treating his servants fairly. God will be after him if he does otherwise. Job would find himself involved in another court case, this time a case in which he is the defendant. God would be the one taking the stand in the heavenly court to bring a charge, and Job knows that being found guilty would lead to the court's determining to take action that will issue in trouble coming to him. It is the set of assumptions about how life works out in the world (that is, wrongdoing leads to punishment) that Job affirms just as much as his friends do— which is why he is so full of protest that it is not how things are working out in his experience. At least, he affirms this set of assumptions for the sake of argument. One might suspect that he is the kind of upright person who does what is right because it is right, not just because he is afraid of getting caught (which is the adversary's cynical view).

The other point is his theological insight, that his servants are the same kind of being as he is. For all their difference in status, what they have in common as human beings is more significant. Master and servant were formed by the one God. Recognizing this fact would have subverted the development of the Western slave trade and the practice of slavery.

Job can claim similar integrity in relation to other people who belong to his broader family or have a moral claim on it. He talks first about the "poor," who are people who do not have land. Maybe they have lost it in the same way as people who have become servants, but they have not found themselves a place in a family in the manner of servants. Naomi and Ruth are people in this position when they arrive in Bethlehem; they are forced to rely on grain they can glean and/or on the generosity of a Job-like man such as Boaz. They are thus also the "needy," people who do not have enough to eat, a place to live, a healthcare plan, or attire suitable for the winter. Job has made it possible for them to have warm, wool clothing.

It is quite a claim on Job's part that he has not held back from their "want" or desire, that which will delight them or give them pleasure. He does not refer merely to their needs. Maybe his reference to not eating alone hints at the significance of this claim. A poor person doesn't want someone merely to hand over a meal that the person goes off to eat alone. People want to belong, and eating with others is a mark of belonging. When our church makes dinner for the people in a local homeless shelter, we are expected simply to serve them the meal, not to eat with them. There is something wrong with the system, however, when it requires the meal to work that way.

One can imagine that widows and orphans would especially long to belong. They are examples of the poor and needy, and Naomi and Ruth again illustrate what it is like to be in their position. Widows and orphans are people who have fallen out of the social structure of the family through the death of a husband and father, and Job can say he has recognized the claim they have on him. Indeed, over decades (he can claim) he has made sure they were looked after, so that the widow's eyes have

not failed as they have looked in vain for something to give her
hope. Job is aware that there is another aspect to the vulnerability of the orphan. A man of prestige and power such as Job
always has friends among the gathering of the elders at the city
gate. Shaking the hand against him perhaps implies some legal
gesture like raising one's hand in an oath to tell the truth; a
powerful man can commit perjury and rob someone by means
of legal processes through having friends on the jury. The evidence of Job's integrity in this connection is the blessing Job
receives from the needy, the way they express their appreciation for his care. If you doubt whether I speak the truth, Job
implies, just ask them.

JOB 31:24–40

The Way I Have Walked (III)

24 If I have made gold my confidence
    or said of fine gold, "my security,"
25 if I celebrate because my resources are great,
    because my hand has found much,
26 if I have seen the light when it shines,
    the bright moon proceeding,
27 and my mind succumbed in secret,
    and my mouth kissed my hand,
28 that, too, would be waywardness calling for mediation,
    because I would have been deceiving God above.

29 If I celebrate the calamity of someone who has repudiated me
    or thrill when evil has found him—
30 but I have not given my mouth to committing an offense,
    to asking for his life by a curse.
31 If the men in my tent have not said,
    "If only someone had not been full of his meat." . . .
32 No stranger lodges in the street;
    I open my doors to the road.
33 If I covered my rebellion like Adam,
    hiding my waywardness in my heart,
34 because I would fear the great crowd,
    and the contempt of families terrifies me,
    so that I keep quiet and do not go outside. . . .

³⁵ I wish I had someone listening to me;
    here is my mark—Shadday should reply to me,
    the one who contends with me should write a document.
³⁶ I would surely carry it on my shoulder,
    bind it on me like a crown.
³⁷ I would tell him the number of my steps,
    present it as to a ruler.

³⁸ If my land cries out against me
    and its furrows weep together,
³⁹ if I have eaten its yield without silver
    and made its owners breathe out their life,
⁴⁰ instead of wheat may thistle come up,
    instead of barley, stinkweed.

The words of Job have come to an end.

A year or two ago, a friend of mine lost his wife after she had been ill for a while, and to my horror I was aware of feeling something like satisfaction at this event because my wife had recently died after being ill for many years. Somehow my loss seemed less unfair because someone else had had the same experience. It was a horrible response to have, though it is a sufficiently well-recognized one that there is a word for it: schadenfreude, pleasure at someone else's misfortune. (It is interesting that English didn't have a word for it, so we had to borrow the German word.)

Many of Job's claims about his integrity in this chapter make me uncomfortable because they make me wonder whether I can make the claims he makes. I assume I will not be the only person who reacts this way, which is one reason for giving them extended space in this commentary. It might be that Job is deluding himself about his claims, though that would be a risky thing since they form the basis for his case against God. Furthermore, the book's whole argument would be imperiled if there was too much self-whitewashing in this chapter. To put it another way, this extended claim to integrity makes explicit to the readers of the book that Job has not yielded an inch to the friends' argument that his suffering must be the result of his sin. He shows he is aware that people might say he is spreading whitewash when he refers to his awareness that consequences would follow if he were rebellious or wayward and concealed the fact. What sort of rebellion or waywardness he has in mind is presumably the kind of acts that the rest of the chapter describes. The first disincentive with regard to secret wrongdoing to which he refers is public opinion. No one in the village would want to have anything to do with him. But he goes on to declare his desire for God to listen to him and respond to his claims, which suggests that he has no more to fear from God than from his community. He imagines God giving him a written deposition, which Job would then flaunt—perhaps because it would be blank, perhaps because it would be manifestly false. And he imagines it therefore providing him the chance to get back at God.

We cannot evaluate Job's claims regarding his own life (though the opening of the book has already given us God's evaluation), but we can see where they make us feel uncomfortable. The one that makes me the most uncomfortable is when Job claims in this last section of the chapter not to have rejoiced at the fall of someone else. Job believes he is not guilty of schadenfreude. Admittedly he nuances the claim in a way that suggests a different challenge. As I write, people are debating the killing of Osama bin Laden, which occurred two weeks ago. The media have shown films of crowds cheering and letting off fireworks in Times Square or outside the White House, and they have related the arguments between pundits who think it is quite proper to celebrate because justice has been done and others who think it is unseemly. It looks as if Job's would be the second stance. Satisfaction that a dangerous leader can no longer attack us might be fine; celebration at an act of vengeance would be a different matter.

We noted in connection with chapter 27 that the word for repudiation is often translated "hate" but that it does not refer to a mere emotion but rather to an action. It suggests turning one's back on people, having nothing to do with them, and opposing them. Job knows what it is like to be on the receiving end of such treatment when he does not deserve it, and he has known the experience of seeing trouble come to people who have taken that stance to him. He could be forgiven for thinking that God might be punishing them for their wrongdoing.

Job agrees with the friends that God does and should bring trouble to people who do wrong, but he declares that he has not felt joy or excitement when that has happened.

Furthermore, in case anyone wondered, neither has he been involved in bringing about calamity to them. He does not quite say that he has not even prayed that God would punish them, but he does say that he has not cursed them. There is a close link between prayer and cursing or blessing, but there is a difference. Prayer assumes that God is going to make the decision about what happens, and the Psalms give the impression that you can pray for anything, including the punishment of people who are treating you wrongly. Cursing and blessing assume that God has given over some power in the world to human beings, so that words of cursing and blessing can have inherent effectiveness—though other parts of Scripture imply that curses will not have an effect if they are uttered against people who are not deserving of a curse. The implication of Job's words is that people who trouble him could not complain if he cursed them, but he has not done so. He recognizes that it would be an offense against what is right.

Rather the opposite, the other people in his "tent" would say (he goes on, taking up a theme from earlier in his statement). As usual, his use of the word "tent" does not imply that he actually lived in one. "Tent" is usually a figurative term for a house, and he often uses the word "house." Here it will make more sense if he is talking about other people who live with him in the village. His peers think he is crazy. He gives food away to everyone and welcomes everyone into his house. They are full of food that comes from him, that he and his own family could have eaten. His own family has to share its living space with these strangers, who were probably not very clean. When Libyan refugees arrived in Tunisia over the past few weeks as I write, Tunisians who were not well-off shared their homes and food with them. "This is how it is; these are our customs," one of them commented. "If there is something to eat, we will eat it together. If there is nothing to eat, we will have nothing together." Many people in the Western world would find such action extraordinary, and so would many people in Job's village, but Job would be able to identify with it.

This last section of Job's declaration actually begins with a claim not to have trusted in his resources, which is quite something for a man who has done as well as Job. It goes on to refer to the temptation to look to the sun and the moon (kissing the hand is perhaps like throwing a kiss). The celestial powers are further potential objects of trust, because other peoples commonly look to them for guidance and treat them as if they determine how life works out on earth. Paying too much attention to them in this way would turn one's adherence to God into deceit. Further, like adultery, it would not be simply a private sin but an action that would implicate the community and thus concern it. The **Torah** speaks of the community's having a responsibility to deal with a person involved in idolatry, and Job's reference to mediation makes the same assumption. The declaration closes with the claim that he has conducted his work life properly. He has not failed to give the land its Sabbath years, to pay his tithes, or to pay his workers properly, thus not imperiling their lives. Job has reviewed his life and can claim to have lived with integrity in every area of it. He is ready to confront God or be confronted by God, and we are ready for the confrontation, so what follows will be a surprise.

JOB 32:1-22

The Angry Young Man

¹These three men ceased replying to Job, because he was in the right in his own eyes. ²But anger flared up in Elihu son of Barachel the Buzite, of the family of Ram. His anger flared up at Job because he thought himself more in the right than God, ³and his anger flared up at his three friends because they did not find a reply although they thought him in the wrong. ⁴Elihu had waited for Job with his words because they were older than him in years, ⁵but when Elihu saw that there was no reply on the lips of the three men, his anger flared up. ⁶So Elihu son of Barachel the Buzite replied:

> I am young in years,
>   and you are old.

For this reason I was afraid and fearful
    of explaining what I know to you.
⁷ I said, "Age should speak;
    abundance of years should make insight known."
⁸ Yet it is the spirit in a mortal,
    the breath of Shadday, that gives understanding.
⁹ It is not the great people who have insight
    or the elders who understand how to make decisions.
¹⁰ Therefore I say, "Listen to me.
    I myself will explain what I know, as well."

¹¹ Yes, I have waited for your speeches;
    I have given ear to your understanding.
    While you searched for things to say,
¹² I attended to you.
    But there: there is no one who has reproved Job;
    none of you has replied to his words.
¹³ Beware lest you say, "We have found insight;
    God must defeat him, not a human being."
¹⁴ He did not set out to me what he had to say,
    and I will not respond to him with your words.

¹⁵ They have collapsed, they have not replied anymore;
    they have let words pass away from them.
¹⁶ Shall I wait, because they do not speak,
    because they have stood still and not replied anymore?
¹⁷ I myself will reply as well with my share;
    I will declare what I know, as well.
¹⁸ Because I am full of things to say;
    the spirit in my insides constrains me.
¹⁹ Yes, my insides are like wine that does not open,
    like skins of new wine that burst.
²⁰ I must speak so that it will relieve me;
    I will open my lips and reply.
²¹ I will surely not show favor to anyone
    or give titles to any person.
²² Because I don't know how to give titles;
    my maker would soon carry me off.

I was a "word child." Indeed, I probably still am, though I am
also a music child and a people child. *A Word Child* is a novel
by Iris Murdoch about a man for whom words are the means of

his redemption or happiness. Words save him. For me, that was so from the beginning, and not because I had the grim family background of the character in the novel. I remember getting in trouble with the public library when I took books out in the morning, read them by the afternoon, and wanted to return them to take out more in the evening. Whereas I would have spent my life working in factories like my father and mother if I had been born a decade earlier than I was, by the time I was born, the sky was the educational limit for ordinary British children. Words could then become not only something I loved to read but something I loved to write. You are the victims.

Elihu is a word child. He loves words, and he loves words for "words"—he uses three different words for "words," which I have translated "speeches," "things to say," and "words." Of course his words are spoken rather than written, which is the more common form that words took in Western culture in before the invention of the printing press. But the function of words still overlaps with the function they have in modern culture. Elihu agrees with the other three friends that words are really important when you are dealing with an experience like Job's, and Job agrees. So for that matter does God, to judge from the words God utters in due course.

Job's three friends have given up words because they have failed to budge Job from his conviction about being in the right. They have collapsed. They therefore implicitly establish the limitations of words, which may be utterly convincing to the speaker but have no impact on the hearer—or may have only negative impact. Proverbs and Ecclesiastes, the other Old Testament books that belong with Job in seeking to offer people insight on life (what are often called Wisdom books), often comment on the pointlessness and danger of words, though their comments deconstruct since the books are full of words. The book of Job, too, is full of words, but it testifies to their uselessness. (When I am asked what I might have done if I were not an Old Testament professor, my favorite answers are that I would have been either a rock-music journalist or a therapist. I now realize that the former—like being a professor—depends on using lots of words, whereas the latter depends more on listening to words rather than talking.)

Elihu doesn't see the irony in his attitude to words. One might have thought that his recognition that the friends' words were useless would make him hesitant to add to them. Instead, he is just like an Old Testament professor. There are many questions about the origin of the Old Testament books and their history that no one knows how to solve. I mentioned one earlier: whether something untoward has happened to the second half of the book of Job, causing the chapters to be in the wrong order. Lots of people have suggested how to put the book into the original order, but this process has not generated agreement on how to do so. It suggests that if the book has been rearranged, we cannot recover the original order, but it doesn't stop us from generating new suggestions. Like Elihu, we find that the failure of other people's theories encourages rather than discourages us in presenting our own.

It looks as if Buz, like Uz, is in Edom, so Elihu is set forward as someone who shares the Edomites' well-known expertise on human insight, a background he also shares with the three friends. Elihu has youth on his side, but he also has youth against him because in a society that respects age, his youth has required him to keep quiet while they spoke, and to do so until they were done. But now they have given up. They believe in their own insight, but they have become reconciled to their inability to win Job over to their way of thinking. God is the only one who will be able to do so. Events will show that they are right that it will take God to change Job's stance, though not in the direction they have in mind.

Elihu "knows" what needs to be said to Job. Twice he refers to what he "knows"; lack of confidence about what one knows is not a common characteristic of youth. A quote attributed to Mark Twain declares, "When I was a boy of fourteen, my father was so ignorant I could hardly stand to have the old man around. But when I got to be twenty-one, I was astonished at how much the old man had learned in seven years." As the bumper sticker says, "Hire a teenager—they know everything." Maybe the author of Job knows there will be young men in the book's audience who at this point are muttering within themselves the kind of argument Elihu uses: "Old people are stuck in their blindness about how things really are." Before God is allowed to appear, the book doesn't want to leave a smidgeon of doubt in the mind of anyone in the audience that all arguments have been presented and that Job is the innocent sufferer.

Yet convention has required Elihu to hold back, and he has been reticent to speak. The story notes four times that his holding back has made him angry with the three friends and with Job for the same reason that causes them to be frustrated with Job. Elihu's anger suggests yet another irony. Anger is another topic about which Proverbs and Ecclesiastes warn. It is fools who get angry, they say. Elihu's claim to share insight is compromised by his anger.

His self-confidence is boosted by theology as well as age. Insight does not come from age. It comes from God's spirit. Oddly enough, that is where Eliphaz located the source of his insight in his first address to Job, but Eliphaz was referring to a special, unusual experience of receiving a message from God, like a prophecy. By "spirit" Elihu means that there is something of the "breath of **Shadday**" in everyone. For "breath" he uses the word that appears in Genesis when it says that God breathed the breath of life into Adam, while "spirit" is the word Genesis used when describing the flood destroying everything that had the spirit of life. It is Elihu's ordinary humanity as a person created in God's image that gives him something to say.

There is another significance about his speaking in terms of spirit. Elihu claims not to be talking about mere intellectual insight. In a sense he does agree with Eliphaz. When the Bible talks about God's spirit, it is referring to a reality that is tumultuous and dynamic, not cool and rational. It enables Samson to kill a lion. Elihu is bursting to speak, and he attributes that compulsion to the activity of God's spirit within him, the spirit God put there at creation. Whether or not Elihu is fooling himself about his insight, he offers a suggestive angle on creation and God's spirit. When God's spirit is active in someone, it is not an add-on from outside but the bringing to fruition of an aspect of the way God made us. It is God who made us people who think up theories about how life works and people who question both our friends' behavior and their authority, but evidently it does not mean we are right every time we do so. God's spirit trumps natural human impulses, abilities, and rationales.

JOB 33:1–33

Pastoral Care That Makes the Sufferer's Position Worse

¹ Nevertheless, do listen to my words, Job;
    give ear to all I have to say.
² Now. I am opening my lips;
    my tongue is speaking in my mouth.
³ My words are the uprightness of my mind;
    my lips are speaking what I know with sincerity.
⁴ The spirit of God made me;
    the breath of Shadday keeps me alive.
⁵ If you can, answer me;
    lay it out before me, take your stand.
⁶ Now. To God, I am the same as you;
    I was taken from clay, as well.
⁷ There. Fear of me should not terrify you;
    pressure from me should not be heavy on you.

⁸ You indeed said in my ears,
    and I have heard the sound of the words:
⁹ "I am innocent, without rebellion;
    I am pure; there is no waywardness in me.
¹⁰ Now. He finds occasions for opposition to me,
    considers me his enemy.
¹¹ He puts my feet in the stocks,
    watches all my ways."
¹² Now. In this you are not in the right; I will reply to you,
    that God is greater than a mortal.
¹³ Why do you contend with him,
    on the grounds that he does not reply to any of
    [a mortal's] words?
¹⁴ Because God speaks once,
    and twice, without him beholding it.
¹⁵ In a dream, a vision in the night,
    when deep sleep falls on people,
    during slumbers in bed,
¹⁶ then he opens the ear of people,
    and in correcting them perturbs them,
¹⁷ to turn a person from an action
    and cover his majesty from a man.
¹⁸ He holds him back from the Pit;
    his life, from crossing the River.

19 He is reproved by pains on his bed,
      constant contention in his bones.
20 His life makes him loathe bread;
      his appetite [makes him loathe] attractive food.
21 His flesh wastes away so that it cannot be seen;
      his bones that could not be seen are laid bare.
22 He draws near to the Pit,
      his life to the bringers of death.
23 If there is an aide by him,
      one messenger from the thousand,
      to declare the person's integrity,
24 and be gracious to him and say,
      "Redeem him from descending to the Pit;
      I have found a ransom":
25 His flesh healthier than his youth,
      he will return to his young days.
26 He will pray to God, and he will accept him;
      he will see [God's] face with a shout.
    So he will restore his faithfulness to the mortal,
27   who will sing to people and say,
      "I offended and twisted what was upright,
      and it was not proper for me.
28 He redeemed me from passing into the Pit;
      my life will see light."

29 There. God does all these things,
      two or three times to a man,
30 to bring his life back from the Pit
      so that the light of life may shine.
31 Pay heed, Job, listen to me;
      be quiet, so that I may speak.
32 If there are things to say, answer;
      speak, because I want you to be in the right.
33 If there are not, you listen to me;
      be quiet, and I will teach you insight.

A woman came to see me a little while ago to talk about an occasion when she had been given pastoral care by some people, and she said the occasion had left her disturbed for years. I knew her to be an intelligent and gifted person but someone lacking in self-confidence, and in the process of these people's

163

pastoring, she realized that her lack of confidence stemmed from a tricky upbringing that included her parents' divorce when she was quite young. The people who were going to pray with her about her personal needs believed that she was possessed by various demons and so spent the evening exorcising them. She found this a disturbing experience, which would be reasonable whatever one believes about the realities it assumes. She also did not find it to be a liberating experience. If anything, over the years that have followed it has held her back in her vision or expectations of God's involvement in her life and in her understanding of the role of the Holy Spirit in our lives.

I'm not sure that the Bible gives us a basis for thinking that demons can possess people who belong to Christ, but if we grant for the sake of argument that this is possible, it looks to me as if nevertheless these people were exercising a ministry that was inappropriate to the woman. Elihu is in an equivalent danger. Actually it was the three friends' danger, too, but Elihu's perspective is both more constructive and more dangerous than theirs, not least in its appeal to the activity of God's spirit in a way that risks manipulation.

Like the friends, Elihu has a theory about how life with God works, especially in the context of suffering. When you are suffering, you may well feel that God is ignoring you, as Job did. God does not ignore us, Elihu says. Rather God speaks to us through our suffering. God is seeking to pull us out of wrong action and thus provide us with a way out of having to face God's majesty or finding that our suffering becomes death. The problem is that people don't listen. It's a plausible theory, but it's an explanation that can make sufferers feel worse if they are trying hard to listen to God and cannot.

Suppose suffering hits you in the form of a serious illness that threatens death. And suppose you are basically a person of integrity, even if you have done something that requires serious divine chastisement. Elihu's theory is that if you are fortunate, you may have a supernatural champion with something like the role that Job has said he longs for or wishes; there are, after all, thousands of them. Elihu thinks, then, in terms of a scene in the cabinet in heaven, though he also speaks of the champion standing by the sufferer's side, so perhaps the idea is that in some sense the sufferer is there at the meeting of the cabinet where his case is being considered (there is a scene rather like this in Zechariah 3). The champion takes the sufferer's side and speaks for him. He thus acts graciously on the sufferer's behalf. The very use of the word "grace" suggests that his action is not based merely on the sufferer's merit. The champion simply appeals for God to "redeem" him because he has found a "ransom." He does not tell us what the ransom is—maybe it is the sufferer's general integrity, which ought to counterbalance the particular wrongdoing that has led to his chastisement, or maybe it is the sufferer's willingness to repent, which has not been mentioned yet but will be manifested in a moment.

Whatever it is, it should mean his full healing. He'll be able to show up at the sanctuary and pray and find acceptance with God there and have his prayer answered. Elihu may not be observing chronological order—possibly the healing will actually follow the prayer. Anyway, the sufferer will see God. It's unusual for the Old Testament to speak in those terms, because it knows that seeing God would imply looking at someone with a brightness a thousand times that of the sun. Maybe it is a metaphor, as when Christians talk about seeing God, and Elihu means the sufferer will have an experience of being in God's presence, or maybe Elihu means he will see God's action—see his healing in response to his prayer. Whereas God has thus been withholding his faithfulness from the sufferer, God will now show it to him once again. So he will be able and will have reason to join in the kind of boisterous acknowledgment of God that the rest of the congregation offers. Instead of being separated from it as he has been in his illness, he'll be able to join in its singing and to add his own testimony to that faithfulness.

So far so good. But now comes the sting in the tail. So far Elihu has commended to Job the kind of stance and practice that is presupposed in the Psalms. When things go wrong in your life, you bring them to God and protest in the way Job has, and you hope for God to respond. When God does so, you bring your testimony to the congregation. But the Psalms hardly ever assume that suffering results from sin. Indeed, they commonly make the kind of protest Job has offered, that one's affliction has happened despite one's faithfulness. The sting in the tail is that Elihu has the sufferer acknowledging the wrong he did that issued in his suffering, notwithstanding the previous integrity of his life. For all his protestations that he has something new to say, Elihu's understanding of Job's position and of how life with God works is not so different from that of the friends. Job is suffering, so he must have sinned, and he needs to repent. Elihu's pastoral ministry parallels that given to the woman I spoke of previously. It may sometimes be appropriate, but taken as a one-size-fits-all theory it is debilitating and leaves its object worse off than he or she was before. Although Elihu starts off by claiming to identify with Job and saying Job has nothing to fear from him, in reality Elihu is just as distanced from Job as the three friends are, and Job has even more to fear from him.

JOB 34:1–30

Is God Not Good or Not Sovereign?

¹ Elihu replied:
² Listen to my words, you men of insight;
    give heed to me, you who have knowledge,
³ because the ear tests words
    [as] the palate tastes something to eat.
⁴ Let's choose a decision for ourselves;
    let's know among ourselves what is good.
⁵ Because Job has said, "I am in the right;
    God has pushed away the case about me.
⁶ As regards the case about me, I declare it false;
    I am fatally wounded by the arrow in me, without my
        having rebelled."
⁷ What man is like Job,
    who drinks scorn like water?
⁸ He travels in cahoots with people who act wickedly,
    and he walks with the faithless,
⁹ because he has said, "It is no use to a man
    when he pleases God."

¹⁰ Therefore, people of understanding, listen to me.
    Far be it for God to act in faithlessness,
    for Shadday to do wrong.

¹¹ Because he requites a person's action to him,
    and in accordance with an individual's walk he makes
        him meet with things.
¹² Assuredly, in truth God does not act faithlessly;
    Shadday does not twist decision making.
¹³ Who gave charge of the earth to him;
    who assigned the world to him, all of it?
¹⁴ If he applies his mind to it, he can gather his spirit
    and his breath to him.
¹⁵ All flesh would expire together,
    and humanity return to the dirt.

¹⁶ So if you have understanding, listen to this,
    give heed to the sound of my words.
¹⁷ Is it really the case that one who repudiates decision
        making is in control?—
    do you declare the faithful, strong one to be faithless?
¹⁸ He is the one who says to a king, "Scoundrel";
    to rulers, "Faithless,"
¹⁹ Who does not show favor to leaders
    and does not recognize the nobility above the poor.
    Because all of them are the work of his hands;
²⁰ suddenly they die,
    in the middle of the night.
    The people are in turmoil, and they pass away;
        they remove a mighty person, not by human hand.

²¹ Because his eyes are on a person's ways;
    he sees all his steps.
²² There is no darkness, there is no deathly shadow,
    for people who do wrong to hide there.
²³ Because he does not set a time for a person
    to go to God for a decision.
²⁴ He shatters strong people without inquiry
    and sets up others in place of them.
²⁵ Thus he recognizes their deeds;
    he overturns them in the night, and they collapse.
²⁶ He chastises them among the faithless
    in a place where people see.
²⁷ Because of the fact that they have turned from following him;
    they have not had regard for any of his ways,

²⁸ so as to cause the cry of the poor to come to him,
   so that he listens to the cry of the lowly.
²⁹ Should he be silent, who can call him faithless?
   —should he hide his face, who can behold him?
   He is over nation and over individual together,
³⁰ to stop the impious person reigning,
   those who ensnare the people.

A student has been blowing fuses to me about having to read books that are full of words like *eschatology* and *pneumatology* and sentences about God's "ontological revelatory self-communication and self-transcendence" or about "supralapsarian-soteriological theater." These books (he says with irony) are noetically confusing. Reading them is like having your mouth full of cotton candy (candy floss, in Britain) instead of food. And the contributions that his fellow students make in class are similar. One of my responses is that students are inclined to think that long words ending with "logy" are a good thing (and of course some such long words are useful as technical terms). Such words sound as if they are saying something impressive, though they tend to dissolve like cotton candy if one asks what they mean.

Elihu's words to Job give us a similar feeling. It's a young man's problem. Maybe like many young men, Elihu is looking for a forum for a speech he has prepared so that he can show people how smart he is. Elihu goes on and on, and you want to interrupt him to scream, "You are not saying anything. You are at least as bad as the friends you criticized." The main burden of this address is simply to reassert the point that the friends made without taking any account of the way it is called into question by what has happened to Job. It must be the case that God acts justly and faithfully. God has power in the world, after all; there is no one else in charge of the world and no one who put God in charge of the world. As well as having a moral nature, God has the power that makes it possible as well as necessary for God to see that the world works in a fair way. Confronted by the question "How can we account for the way bad things happen to good people, if God is good and powerful?" it is possible to risk compromising God's goodness by agreeing that God does do things that look pretty questionable (that would be Job's move, and it is the usual Old Testament move). Or it would be possible to risk compromising God's sovereignty by attributing evil events to Satan and/or to human free will (that is the usual Christian move). Or it would be possible to deny that bad things happen to good people (that is Elihu's move).

His address goes on to focus on the sovereignty of God as one who evaluates rulers and puts them down in the way many stories in the Old Testament show God doing (Kings, Chronicles, and Daniel offer examples). God does not pay rulers more regard than he does ordinary people, and he puts them down in a way that may involve ordinary people but that involves such remarkable events that it is hard to attribute it to mere human action. God does not have to go in for complex inquiry or investigations about what is happening or what to do. God can just do it, and do it publicly, so everyone can see. Therefore when he does not act, no one can validly ask what is going on or challenge him.

So Elihu puts Job in a kind of double bind. We know God is good and sovereign, so Job's account of his experience cannot be correct; and these truths about God rule out his very raising of any questions about God's acts. These acts are by definition God's good and sovereign acts. Therefore there is nothing to discuss. This is fine if you are Elihu, but it leaves Job with nowhere to go with his awareness of what has happened to him and his awareness of the nature of his relationship with God as it was until his calamity overtook him. Nor is Job alone in his dilemma, because it is not only his individual experience that does not square with Elihu's account of God's activity in the world. Elihu's account would be laughable if it were not so serious, and so serious in its implications. Of course it is possible to grant that God puts down evil and acts on behalf of the weak sometimes. But one would have to have one's eyes firmly shut to maintain that this is consistently the case.

Formally, Elihu's addresses differ from those of the three friends by virtue of the fact that his four addresses all come together, even though they are presented as separate units;

he actually speaks longer than any of the three do. A characteristic of Elihu's addresses is the way they directly quote or summarize Job's words. He describes Job as drinking scorn like water, a rather odd way of indicating that (as we might put it) his mocking critique of the friends' teaching pours out of his mouth like a fountain. His brief summary is the claim that Job says you don't gain anything from living in a way that pleases God. That scares Elihu because he thinks it removes the basis for living morally. It also robs him of what he thinks is the key to controlling how his own life works out, and it opens him up to the risk of looking like a fool for living morally.

Elihu does not actually accuse Job of being wicked or faithless. He accuses him of being a fellow traveler with such people because his statements will encourage people to live wicked and faithless lives. It is important for people to believe that God punishes wickedness even if it is not the case, because otherwise what motivation do they have for living good lives? Once again, there is an irony in Elihu's charge, for the starting point of the book is the question of whether Job lives in that way only because it pays. Job has indeed spoken along the lines that Elihu says, and it is his persistence in his commitment to living a life of integrity even though it does not pay that shows he does not live in that way simply because it pays. A major significance of the book is to argue that we live lives that are both good and authentic only if we live our lives this way because they are good and not because of what we get out of it. Its argument is the one Paul will presuppose in Romans 6. In response to the person who asks, "Shall we sin so that grace may abound" Paul does not say, "If you take that attitude, you will find that grace does not abound." Rather he responds by saying, "If you take that attitude, it shows you have not understood anything about my argument so far concerning the purpose of God's redeeming us." Both Job and Paul have to keep underscoring the point because it goes against the grain to accept that God expects us to act righteously no matter what our circumstances or how we are feeling or how people are treating us.

JOB 34:31–35:16

Tested to the Limit

³¹ Because has someone said to God,
   "If I have exalted myself, I will not act corruptly.
³² What I cannot see, teach me yourself;
   if I have done wrong, I will not do so again"?
³³ Is he to requite in the way you think,
   when you have rejected [him]?
Because you, not I, should choose;
   speak what you know.
³⁴ People of understanding say to me,
   a person of insight who listens to me,
³⁵ "Job does not speak with knowledge;
   his words are not with discernment.
³⁶ Would that Job were tested to the limit
   in connection with answers like those of faithless people.
³⁷ Because he adds to his offense,
   he claps in rebellion among us
   and multiplies his words to God."

^{35:1} Elihu spoke again:
² Do you think this is a good decision;
   you say, "I am in the right, not God."
³ If you say, "What use is it to you?"—
   "How do I profit more than from committing an offense?"
⁴ I myself will give you some words in reply,
   and your friends with you.
⁵ Look to the heavens and see;
   behold the skies that are high above you.
⁶ If you have committed an offense, what do you do to him,
   and if your rebellions have been many, how do you
     affect him?
⁷ If you are in the right, what do you give him,
   or what does he receive from your hand?
⁸ Your faithlessness affects a person like yourself;
   your being in the right affects a human being.

⁹ Because of the multitude of oppressions people cry out;
   they cry for help because of the power of the great,

171

¹⁰ but no one says, "Where is God my maker, who gives songs
in the night,
¹¹ who teaches us more than the creatures of the earth,
gives us more insight than the birds in the heavens?"
¹² There they do cry out, but he does not reply,
because of the high-mindedness of faithless people.
¹³ Indeed God does not listen to emptiness;
Shadday does not behold it.
¹⁴ How much less when you say you do not behold him,
your case is before him, and you wait for him,
¹⁵ and now that his anger has paid attention to nothing,
and he has not taken much notice of rebellion.
¹⁶ Job opens his mouth with triviality,
multiplies words without knowledge.

One aspect of the forty-two years during which my first wife
had multiple sclerosis was that it was a time of periodic testing,
or even of continuous testing (but it was also joyful). As she
got to be recurrently tired, or could no longer do things in the
house, or couldn't be very interested in my worries or anxiet-
ies, or could only walk very slowly, or couldn't look after her
personal needs, or couldn't remember things, or got annoyed
with me from time to time, or needed help getting in and out
of bed, or could no longer feed herself, or no longer speak—
how would I cope? My image for it was that it was like weight
training. When I could lift a particular weight, the result wasn't
that I could then give up training. Rather, along came the next
weight, to see if I could lift that one. Sometimes I could feel I
was being tested to the limit. But it meant I grew.

Elihu speaks of people thinking it would be good for Job
to be "tested to the limit." This is exactly what is happening
to Job. The first paragraph above (34:31–37) begins with Elihu
addressing Job about a hypothetical person, but Job himself
is the person Elihu is referring to. Elihu's advice is that Job
needs to acknowledge to God at least the possibility that he
is in the wrong and to undertake to change his ways if necessary. In acknowledging the possibility that he is in the wrong,
he must also recognize that he will need to accept the consequences instead of objecting to the way God is treating him.
If he turns out to be guilty, he surely cannot expect to decide

what happens to him as a punishment. As well as challenging Job to recognize that this is so, Elihu confronts him with what other people (allegedly) say: that Job does not actually have the insight to recognize what is going on between him and God. It is in this connection that they think that Job needs some testing. He talks too much like a faithless person in questioning whether wrongdoing receives its reward (it is obviously in the interests of faithless people to question that truth). They believe that he is a barefaced and enthusiastic rebel against God. That is why he needs to be tested. The irony is that the very process of false accusation that he is experiencing from Elihu and from the (possibly imaginary) people who agree with Elihu is a consequence of a testing that takes Job to the limit.

Elihu goes on to attribute even more astringent words to Job, as if he were asking God whether Job's actions make the slightest difference to God, and whether from Job's own point of view there was any advantage in avoiding sin. It is hard to imagine more skeptical or more hopeless words. They imply that there is simply no point of contact between Job and God. Job doesn't make any difference to God; God doesn't make any difference to Job. Humanity and God live in separate, hermetically sealed worlds. Elihu is by no means in complete disagreement with the view that he attributes to Job, but he draws different conclusions. Yes, God is on high, and nothing we do can really affect God, but our faithlessness or faithfulness does affect other people. It is a clever and profound half-truth, strangely congenial to a liberal culture where religion might seem neither here nor there and where loving your neighbor and being socially involved were what counted.

A Jew or a Christian might respond with gratitude that we know that our relationship with God is like that of a parent with a child. While there is a world of difference between parent and child, and the parent has all sorts of interests and activities that the child does not share, nevertheless parents care passionately about their children's lives and actions and are deeply affected by them. It continues to be so when the children are adults. So it is with God, whose relationship with us is like that of parents with their adult sons and daughters (not that of parents with their little children)—though still with the kind of authority that parents have in relation to adult children in a traditional society. The book of Job might make the point in a different way. It does not see God and Job as father and son or speak of the relationship as one of love. But it does see them as master and servant, and even though there is also a world of difference between masters and servants, that relationship is one of mutual commitment and involvement. What the servant does matters to the master and is of real use to him. The scene in heaven has shown the particular way Job's behavior indeed matters to God; God stakes his reputation on it. While Elihu is right that Job's conduct matters considerably to other human beings, it matters to God, too.

To Elihu, it seems misguided to have high expectations of God's involvement in the world. He closes with some alternative partial explanations for God's failure to intervene in the world when the oppressed cry out as powerful people exercise their power over them. God does not intervene simply because people are in pain. Sometimes the problem is that people are crying out, but not to God. They do not bring God into the picture, the God who is their maker (even if they now make no difference to him), the God who gives them songs to sing in the night (in other words, who enables them to sing in praise even when the circumstances are gloomy), and the God who gives them an understanding of how life works.

The Old Testament provides some instances of people crying out yet not bringing God into the picture. The Israelites in Egypt cried out, but it does not say they cried out to God or referred to God. The Israelites in the wilderness cried out to Moses, not to God. The Judahites in exile in Babylon referred to God; they complained that God paid no attention to their situation and needs. But they, too, were talking *about* God, not *to* God. In each case, God responds, but Elihu's point might be valid: that people who do not bring God into the picture or complain to God in the way the Psalms model can hardly complain if God does not respond.

Does Elihu imply that Job has not brought God into the picture? Certainly Job has sometimes simply lamented or has referred to God rather than spoken to God, yet he has often addressed God. But Elihu goes on to another reason for God's

174

not responding to people's cries, which he thinks does catch Job. God may not respond to the cries of the oppressed when they are also the faithless. Not all oppressed people are simply the victims of wickedness. They may be its perpetrators, too. Job complains that God pays no attention to his case, no matter how long he waits like a suppliant waiting for the king to act. When there is oppression around, God ought to show some anger. Elihu's comment is that God indeed pays no attention to cases that have no substance. Job is talking rubbish.

JOB 36:1–25

The God Who Whispers in Our Ears

¹ Elihu again spoke:
² Wait for me a little, and I will explain to you,
   because there are yet words to be said for God.
³ I will bring my knowledge from far away,
   and I will ascribe faithfulness to my maker.
⁴ Because in truth my words are not false;
   the one who is with you is upright in knowledge.

⁵ There: God is strong, but he does not reject the one
   who is strong in inner might.
⁶ He does not let the faithless live,
   but gives the decision for the lowly.
⁷ He does not hold back his eyes from faithful people,
   but with kings on a throne,
   he seats them forever, and they are on high.
⁸ If people are bound in chains,
   caught in the bonds of lowliness,
⁹ he declares to them what they have done,
   and their acts of rebellion, that they acted big.
¹⁰ He opens their ear to correction
   and says how they should turn from wickedness.
¹¹ If they listen and serve,
   they will complete their days in good fortune,
   their years in happiness.
¹² But if they do not listen, they will cross the River;
   they will expire without knowledge.

¹³ But the impious of mind lay up anger;
    they do not cry for help when he binds them.
¹⁴ They die in youth,
    their life through the holy ones.
¹⁵ He delivers the lowly in their lowliness
    and opens their ear in their oppression.
¹⁶ Indeed, he has drawn you away from the jaws of distress,
    to a spacious place where there is no constraint instead,
    and what is laid on your table is full of richness.

¹⁷ You are full of the judgment due to the faithless person;
    judgment and decision making take hold of you.
¹⁸ Because beware lest someone draw you away with mockery;
    a large amount of ransom money must not turn you
    aside.
¹⁹ Will your wealth make you ready so that you are not in
    distress,
    and all your mighty efforts?
²⁰ Do not long for the night,
    when peoples leave where they are.
²¹ Beware, do not turn to wickedness,
    because you have chosen this rather than lowliness.
²² There: God is glorious in his power;
    who is a teacher like him?
²³ Who has prescribed his way for him;
    who has said, "You have done wrong"?

²⁴ Be mindful that you should exalt what he does,
    which people have sung about.
²⁵ All humanity has seen it;
    a mortal looks from afar.

A young man comes to see me from time to time to discuss what is going on between him and God. He used to seem depressed, but the depression lifted when he came to acknowledge that he was attracted to other men rather than to women. He got involved in a number of same-sex relationships, then decided that while he didn't have to feel guilty about his orientation, he did have to foreswear what amounted to promiscuity in his relationships. But living celibately was tough, too, and more recently he had (as he put it) "fallen" again into the lifestyle he had given up. But he had a sense that God was "following" him into places where he went and was "watching" him—not in a hostile way, but simply by virtue of being there. He knew he had to go back to the celibate practice he had abandoned. (I'm not here presupposing an answer to the broader ethical question about same-sex relationships of a committed, covenantal kind; it was the involvement in more short-term, passing relationships that raised the ethical question, as it would in the case of heterosexual relationships.)

While Elihu has a young man's boorishness, he is not totally deluded when he claims to offer insight that the friends lack, and his talk about God's "following" us and "watching" us (to use that other young man's words) when we "fall" into wrongdoing is worth reflection. Job has spoken of God's creation of him as an expression of God's commitment, of God's love, but he can't see any commitment or love in the way God is relating to him now. He has spoken of the way God then watched over him, and he knows God is still watching over him, but it now seems a negative kind of watching.

Elihu knows of the truth expressed in 2 Peter 3, that God doesn't want anyone to perish but wants everyone to come to repentance. That statement became a football kicked between Calvinists and Arminians, which is a shame because it expresses a truth to encourage us, whether or not we are people who need to do some repenting at the moment. Elihu knows that God watches over us like a father or mother who is more interested in seeing us pull back from wrongful styles of life than in chastising us for continuing to be involved in them. Admittedly, God is also willing to go in for chastisement if necessary. God is also like a master who has an interest in whether we are doing the jobs he wants done, a sovereign who has an interest in our loyalty and commitment, or a teacher who has an interest in the students taking notice of what the teacher says.

Elihu is not concerned here with outrageously wicked people, the people he calls the impious who don't cry out to God when trouble comes to them, who are storing up divine wrath for themselves. He is concerned with people who belong to the ranks of the faithful but who fall to some particular wrongdoing. He speaks of them as the lowly—they are ordinary people without power. People who are lowly in this objective sense may not be lowly in the sense of meek, though it can happen. Similarly, people in positions of power may not also be proud, but it's hard to be both powerful and meek.

So faithful people can act big, and God may thus need to pull them down from their exaltation, but God does not simply destroy them. God "opens their ear" to draw them back to "listening and serving," the submissive attitude to God (and to other people?) that is involved in a lowliness that means meekness of attitude and not merely powerlessness in society.

There are two aspects to students' learning: the teacher speaking and the student hearing. The interface between these two is a mystery. As a teacher I say the same thing to a number of students; some get it, but others do not. My big challenge is getting them to open their ears. Merely speaking clearly may not achieve this end. Last weekend my ears got blocked with wax, as happens every few years. Until I had managed to soften the wax and syringe it out, people were speaking clearly to me, but I was not hearing them. Elihu's point is that God does not settle merely for speaking clearly. To put it in the terms of Jeremiah 31, it is not enough to inscribe with total clarity on stone tablets God's teaching about worshiping **Yahweh** alone and not making images and keeping the Sabbath. This teaching has to be written into people's minds. When that happens, we act on it. The great mystery is how to achieve that writing. Elihu declares that God knows about this challenge and meets it. Maybe God simply gets closer to people's ears so that they can't miss his words, as I needed people to get closer to mine when they were full of wax. People then hear God's correction. Elsewhere that word suggests action that chastises (as in our euphemism "correctional facility"), but here the word is explicated by the second part of the line, in which God says that they must turn from wickedness (as happened at the end of the poem in chapter 28).

Elihu goes on to apply his insight to Job. God has been drawing him away from the jaws of distress. The verb is a suggestive one; it is often translated "entice" or "allure." It invites us to imagine God's whispering in a person's ear: "Come on, you know that what you are doing isn't right, and it isn't wise. Stop it!" The expression for "distress" also means "straits" or "narrowness," and Elihu works with that image. God wants us to be in a place with elbow room, not one that is constrained. The image suggests a good life, and it connects with the idea of luxury, taken up in the picture of a table groaning with good food. By such speaking God opens up the way to delivering the lowly in their lowliness. The alternative to spaciousness is that they have to cross the River earlier than they might have done, that they never learn the lessons about life that they need to learn. They die in youth through the holy ones (an odd phrase, maybe referring to the supernatural agents through whom God acts).

Elihu sees Job in the position of someone to whom God acts with this pastoral care to pull him out of his uncharacteristic wrongdoing. That is why he is fully experiencing the judgment due to faithless people, why he is the victim of divine decision making. He is in danger of mocking people like Elihu who can interpret his position to him, and he must not think that his wealth can somehow buy his way out of his situation, nor must he give into the temptation to join the wrongdoers who do their work under cover of night ("If I am being treated as a wrong-doer, I might as well act like one"). While Elihu's illuminating description of how God exercises pastoral care is irrelevant to Job insofar as God is not in the position of needing to wean Job from wrongdoing, his comments about that temptation are in line with what we know from the beginning of the story.

JOB 36:26–37:24

The Awe-Inspiring Creator

²⁶ There: God is great, and we cannot know—
   of the number of his years there is no finding out.
²⁷ Because he draws up the drops of water
   that distill as rain in his mist,
²⁸ which the skies pour down,
   dispense upon humanity as a shower.
²⁹ Further, can one understand the spreading of cloud,
   the thunders from his shelter?
³⁰ There: he spreads his lightning over it;
   he uncovers the roots of the sea.

³¹ Because by these things he governs peoples,
     gives food in abundance.
³² He covers over his hands with lightning,
     and commands it against its mark.
³³ His thunder tells of him,
     his angry passion against wrongdoing.

³⁷:¹ Indeed at this my heart trembles
     and leaps from its place.
² Listen, listen to the raging of his voice,
     to the rumbling that comes out from his mouth.
³ Beneath the entire heavens he lets it loose,
     and his lightning over the corners of the earth.
⁴ After it, his voice roars;
     he thunders with his majestic voice.
     He does not hold them back when his voice makes itself
         heard;
⁵ God thunders with his voice in wonders.
     He does great things that we cannot know,
⁶ when he says to the snow, "Fall on the earth."
     The downpour of rain is his mighty downpour of the rains.
⁷ He sets a seal on every person's hand
     so that everyone may acknowledge what he does,
⁸ and the beast comes into its lair,
     settles down in its den.
⁹ The tempest comes out of the chamber, the cold from
     the driving winds.
¹⁰ By God's breath he gives ice,
     and the expanse of water is something frozen.
¹¹ He also loads the clouds with moisture,
     scatters his lightning thundercloud,
¹² And it turns around and around by his directions,
     so that [the clouds] do all that he commands them
     over the face of the earthly world.
¹³ Either for a chastisement or for his earth,
     or for commitment—he makes them happen.

¹⁴ Give ear to this, Job;
     stand and consider God's wonders.
¹⁵ Do you know how God lays things upon them,
     how the lightning from his thundercloud shines out?

¹⁶ Do you know about the balancing of the clouds,
    the wonders of the one who is perfect in knowledge,
¹⁷ you whose clothes become hot
    when the land is still because of the south wind?
¹⁸ Could you spread the skies with him,
    hard like a mirror of cast metal?
¹⁹ Make known to us what we are to say to him;
    we cannot lay it out because of the darkness.
²⁰ Is he to be told that I shall speak;
    has someone said that he is to be informed?
²¹ But now, people cannot look at the light
    when it is bright in the skies.
After the wind has passed and cleared them,
²² the gold comes from the north
    (about God, who is wondrous in splendor).
²³ The Almighty: we have not reached him,
    great in power and decision making.
²⁴ Therefore people revere him;
    none of the insightful of mind see him.

The window by my desk looks out over our patio, where I can see geraniums starting to bloom, blue jays coming to bathe in the fountain, and squirrels trying to remember where they stored their nuts. A plant of basil sits on a table and will provide the leaves to make more pesto when we have finished the first batch. There are two or three pots of impatiens flowers of different colors, with their amazing tolerance for shade and neglect. This afternoon the sun will reach our side of the building, and toward evening its light will shine through the trees, glinting off the leaves that get thicker day by day. It is enough to make an urban creature like me rejoice in the wonder of creation.

My wonder at creation bears more relation to nineteenth-century Romanticism than to the wonder at creation that appears in the Bible. Elihu's wonder at creation compares with the wonder that features in the Psalms. What strikes him and the psalm writers about creation is not the gentleness of a brook or the delicate beauty of a snowflake but creation's awe-inspiring magnitude and energy. It is these facts about creation that undergird Elihu's opening observation about God's greatness. Elihu is not specific about what it is that we do not know—maybe the magnitude of God's greatness, maybe the fact that follows, the number of God's years. Elihu does not imply that God has a finite number of years. Rather his point is that God the creator has obviously been around longer than creation, so that the awe-inspiring impressiveness of creation generates in us an awe-inspiring awareness of God's greatness. When people try to prove the existence of God, they sometimes argue from the nature of creation—someone must have brought the world into existence. The evidence that creation was designed implies it had a designer. Elihu is not trying to prove that God exists; in a traditional society this would seem an odd thing to try to do. People knew that God existed. Elihu's concern is to get people to draw the right conclusions from what they know.

It's typical of the Old Testament that it is rain and storm that particularly impress people about nature. Elihu goes on to indicate two reasons, neither of them as significant for the average person from London or Seattle as they are for someone from the Middle East or California. One is that rain is so important to the growing of food and therefore to human survival, and it cannot be taken for granted. The other is that when it comes, it often does so in frighteningly powerful, violent storms, accompanied by thunder and lightning. In the words of the cryptically expressed verse 13, the rain can be for chastisement, or it can be an expression of God's **commitment** to the world.

Elihu's interesting starting point, however, is that he evidently knows how our water supply goes around in circles. The Old Testament often portrays the earth's water supply as contained in reservoirs behind the vault of the sky, which holds the waters back from flooding the earth, or as contained in subterranean reservoirs that bubble up in springs. But Old Testament writers have also worked out that water evaporates from oceans and lakes and eventually returns to earth as rain, and know that it is God who makes this happen. Ecclesiastes comments on the same phenomena and takes them as a sign of the depressing truth that everything in human life and in the world goes around in circles, but Elihu is impressed by this process in nature.

He likewise emphasizes God's involvement in the storm. God fills his hand with lightning bolts and then commissions them to hit their target, like a soldier with a rocket launcher. The storm is his means of exercising government in the world; it expresses his passionate anger against wrongdoing. The effect of snow and rain on humanity is to seal everyone up at home and to keep the animals at home too. (In London or Seattle, if you stayed in because of the rain, you would never go out; but in California they cancel a soccer game if it rains, and people don't come to church because they are afraid to drive in the wet.) In a strange way this means they are acknowledging God. The fierce summer heat of the sun, when the hot wind blows off the desert and the sky is as hard as iron, has the same effect; it too keeps people indoors.

Elihu's point becomes explicit when he asks Job to tell him what, then, we are to say to God. It is not that we cannot know or relate to God but that we cannot do what Job has been doing. The fact that we are in the dark concerning questions about why God makes things work out (or not work out) in our lives as they do does not mean we can press God for answers and expect to receive them. Creation shows that God is too big for us to be able to tell God how to run the world, and it reminds us that we can hardly even appear before God to ask such questions and offer God such advice. If we cannot look the sun in the eye, we can hardly look God in the eye. Insightful people focus on revering and submitting to God rather than expecting to show up to see him.

The surprise about Elihu's argument is that it is close to the one God will put forward in the next two chapters. As it is often thought that the third round of speeches between Job and his friends has been subject to some disruption, it is often thought that Elihu's addresses are a later addition to the book than the speeches of Job and his friends. Again I am not convinced that this is so (though it does not bother me if it is). A major reason for drawing this conclusion is the way Elihu's addresses anticipate God's and the way God rebukes the original three friends but not Elihu. But Elihu's anticipating God's address would be a reason for God not to rebuke him. It acts as a spoiler for God's address, in a positive fashion. Elihu starts to get us thinking in God's way, or at least introduces the idea of thinking from God's angle.

JOB 38:1–15

The God Who Commands the Dawn

¹ Yahweh replied to Job from the tempest:
² Who is this who darkens purpose by words without
   knowledge?
³ Fasten on your armor like a man, will you,
   so that I can ask you and you can make known to me.

⁴ Where were you when I founded the earth?—
   tell, if you have understanding.
⁵ Who set its dimensions, since you will know,
   or who stretched a line over it?
⁶ On what were its bases sunk,
   or who cast its corner stone,
⁷ when the morning stars resounded together
   and all the divine beings shouted?

⁸ Or [who] shut the sea in with doors;
   when it gushed from the womb, it came out,
⁹ when I made cloud its clothing,
   thundercloud its blanket,
¹⁰ decreed my limit for it,
   set a bar and doors,
¹¹ said, "You may come as far as this but not go further;
   here [the limit] is set for the swelling of your waves"?

¹² Since your days began, have you commanded morning,
   made known to the dawn its place,
¹³ for it to seize the earth by the corners
   so that faithless people shake out of it?
¹⁴ It turns like clay [pressed by] a seal
   so that [its features] stand out like a garment.
¹⁵ From faithless people their light holds back
   and their high arm breaks.

On some people's calculations, the world is due to end today. If you are reading this book, it didn't end, or, alternatively, you and I were left behind. I am pretty confident it won't end, though the basis for my confidence is different from that presupposed by the amused media reporting on the expectation.

184

The Day of the Lord is going to arrive one day, and Jesus is going to appear, but the calculations that identify today as the day are false. Indeed, any such calculations are based on false premises. If I were God, and it happened that today was due to be the day, I would be tempted to change the date to put mortals in their place. Alternatively, if today was not due to be the day, I would be tempted to change it to today (or at least to arrange for an earthquake, preferably somewhere harmless), to put the skeptical and amused people in their place.

God is the one who commands morning and tells dawn when to break, the one who founded the earth in the first place, and God will be the one who will act to transform it. God is also the one who deals with creation in a way that responds to human faithlessness, amusement, and stupidity. Job's own experience has made him question this idea and critique the way God's purpose works out in the world. God declares that Job does not know what he is talking about and returns Job's challenge to debate the question.

Speaking out of the tempest would be awe inspiring but in a strange way reassuring, partly because it is characteristic of the way God often speaks in the Old Testament (for instance to Ezekiel). There is no mistaking God's speaking when God speaks in that way. Further, the one who speaks is **Yahweh**, God as he made himself known to Israel, another reminder that although the story of Job is dramatically set in Edom and does not refer to other distinctive features of God's dealing with Israel such as the exodus and the **covenant**, the real God whom Israel knew is the God under discussion in the book. The people who wrote and read the book were members of the people of Yahweh, who agonize about the nature of God's relationship with them and their relationship with God. Further, while for the purposes of argument the book mostly looks at these questions without talking about those distinctive features of God's relationship with Israel and confines itself to the way anyone can see that life works out, having God appear shows how in the end the book recognizes the limits of what can be said on that basis. God's appearing is an idea that belongs in the **Torah** and the Prophets, not in the books that focus on more empirical insight, but eventually the book of Job cannot do without it.

So God appears and responds to Job, but the content of God's response is nothing like what one might have expected. Indeed, we noted in connection with Elihu's closing address, it says the same kind of thing that Elihu (and for that matter the three friends) had said. It points Job to the nature of creation and infers that we must accept our ignorance about many aspects of God's work in the world. God's address goes much further in spelling out the significance of this point, but it continues to work within the framework of what anyone can see. In other contexts, confronted by the question of why bad things happen to good people, an Israelite might have answered, "I don't know, but what Yahweh did with Israel at the exodus, and what Yahweh has been doing with Israel since, and the way Yahweh responded to prayers for my mother when she was sick, makes me able to go on trusting in Yahweh even though bad things do happen to good people" (as Christians carry on trusting in God because the significance of what God did in Christ and what God has done for the church enables us to do so). But suppose that for some reason that appeal is not available or does not work—suppose the exodus seems a long time ago? Maybe looking at creation can have the same effect, though its message will be more complex than Job might have expected.

God points out the obvious fact that Job was not present at creation and notes the way God went about this building project. God was like a man building a house; perhaps the idea is that God was building a house to live in, which makes us think of the temple but also of the cosmos as a whole as God's home. As a house builder, God makes sure that this home has secure foundations. God likely speaks metaphorically. Job has implied that the world is not securely founded; to put it in the terms that Psalm 11 uses, it is as if the moral foundations of human life are destroyed. In that psalm it is faithless people who are destroying them. In Job, it is as if God has not given human life a proper foundation. God here claims to have done so at the beginning and notes how the very stars and the divine beings recognized the wonder of God's creative work. The divine beings are the members of the heavenly cabinet whom we met in chapter 1. The stars, too, are the entities through which God's purpose is achieved in the world. The implication is that the stars and heavenly beings were happy enough with the evidence that God could formulate a purpose and implement it in such a way as to give human life a secure foundation. Is Job more discerning than they?

Second, this process of creation involved setting a limit to the power of dangerous and dynamic forces in creation. The sea is a common Old Testament symbol for such forces; its tumultuous power provides a vivid illustration and embodiment of them. The frightening power of a tsunami provides us with an example. From time to time, the sea's dynamic power gets out of hand; but in principle, God made sure it was under control. God also speaks about the dynamic power of the waters that come from above, the danger of cloudburst and flood. In principle God has also made sure that this power is under control, held back behind the sky and the clouds and generally denied the possibility of flooding the world.

Third, the process of creation involved establishing the rhythm of day and night. In his book *Orthodoxy* (New York: Lane, 1909, chapter 4), G. K Chesterton wondered whether the sun did not rise every morning of its own accord: "It is possible that God says every morning, 'Do it again' to the sun; and every evening, 'Do it again' to the moon." God affirms that this is indeed so. God gives orders to the morning. In the present context, God's point is then that there is a relationship between the daily dawning of light in the world and the exposing of wrongdoers in the world. Night is the natural time for wrongdoing, but at morning the folds in the mountains become exposed like the folds in a garment, and wrongdoers get shaken out of their hiding places as spiders or crumbs get shaken out of a garment. So with the dawn faithless people lose the light they like (that is, what other people call darkness), and they can no longer exercise their violent power in order to do wrong.

What God is doing here is preaching a sermon on creation that applies the significance of creation to the question at hand, the question whether God is executing his purpose in the world properly. God's account of creation recalls Genesis 1 in that it talks about matters such as the making of the world, the stars, the waters constrained by the sky, the separating of sea and land, and the sequence of night and morning. But at each point, like a good preacher, God does not merely describe how something happened but also draws out its implications for its audience—here an audience of one, plus people like us who listen in on the conversation.

JOB 38:16–38

On Accepting Your Ignorance

¹⁶ Have you come to the springs of the sea
   or walked through the extent of the deep?
¹⁷ Have the gates of death opened to you,
   or can you see the gates of deathly shadow?
¹⁸ Have you comprehended the expanses of the earth?—
   Tell, if you know it all.
¹⁹ Where is the way to where light dwells, and darkness—
   where is its place,

²⁰ that you may take it to its territory
   and understand the paths to its home?
²¹ You know, because you were coming to birth then,
   and the number of your years is many.

²² Have you come to the storehouses of snow,
   or can you see the storehouses of hail,
²³ which I have reserved for the time of trouble,
   for the day of people meeting in battle?
²⁴ Where is the way to where lightning disperses,
   or where the east wind is scattered over the earth?
²⁵ Who cut a channel for the torrent
   and a way for the bolt of thunder,
²⁶ to rain on land with no people,
   wilderness with no one in it,
²⁷ to satisfy the devastating devastation
   and make a crop of grass flourish?

²⁸ Does rain have a father,
   or who fathered dewdrops?
²⁹ From whose womb did the ice come out—
   the frost from the heavens, who fathered it,
³⁰ when waters harden like stone
   and the surface of the deep freezes?

³¹ Can you tie bonds to Pleiades
    or loose the cords of Orion?
³² Can you lead out Mazzaroth at its time
    or lead out the Bear with its children?
³³ Do you know the laws of the heavens,
    or can you establish its authority on earth?
³⁴ Can you lift up your voice to the cloud
    so that a flood of waters may cover you?
³⁵ Can you send off shafts of lightning so that they go
    and say to you, "Here we are!"?
³⁶ Who put insight in the ibis,
    or who gave understanding to the cockerel?
³⁷ Who can give an account of the skies by means of insight
    and tilt the water skins in the heavens,
³⁸ when dirt has poured into a mass
    and clods are made to stick together?

In my seminary in England we once produced a dramatic version of the story of Job; I was the screenwriter, and one of my colleagues was the director. She wanted to have God appearing on stage during the dialogues between Job and his friends, silently reaching out his embrace to Job to reassure Job of his presence and concern for him as he went through his ordeal. But I wouldn't let her do so, because there is no hint of it in the book. I guess it would get in the way of the book's point in more than one sense. Many people who go through Job's kind of experience do not have a sense of God's presence or concern. Further, the adversary would have been able to complain that God had compromised the test. The point was to see whether Job would stay faithful if God's blessings disappeared. The test depended on the absolute toughness of what happened to Job. God *was* absent, and Job needed to *experience* God's absence. God had to be tough.

The toughness continues when God finally speaks to Job. There is no expression of sympathy with Job's suffering. Instead, God puts Job in his place, and does so with sarcasm: "Oh yes, you will understand everything about creation, won't you, Job, because you have been around for such a long time!" The first paragraph in the translation above draws Job's attention to the fact that he knows nothing about the depths or breadth of the created world, their bounds, and what lies beyond them. He thus knows nothing about the realm of death and darkness that lies beyond the realm of life and light. These are topics on which he has frequently expostulated. The book of Job uses the word *darkness* more than any other book in the Old Testament, and especially in connection with death. When you die, they put you in a tomb and put a rock on its mouth, and you lie there in the darkness. It is indeed a place of "deathly shadow." That phrase represents one word in Hebrew, another word that comes more often in Job than anywhere else. It looks as if it combines the words "shadow" and "darkness"; that would likely be the connotation it conveyed to people. Job has spoken as if he knows about death and knows about how it would be preferable to his present life, but really he doesn't know. He knows what happens to our bodies in their tombs, but there is some other sense in which dying means we go to the realm of death and of deathly shadow, some other dimension where we are in the realm of death. Job has not gone through its gates to check things out there, so what does he know and what was he doing pontificating on the subject?

Second, God is the lord of snow, hail, storm, rain, frost, and ice. These are resources that God has under control and that God directs. They do not happen randomly. God draws Job's attention to two aspects of the purposeful way God uses them. One relates to historical events such as battles, which are sometimes decided by weather (Joshua 10 gives an example, when God rains hailstones on an army). The other is that rain sometimes falls in wilderness areas where no one lives, areas characterized by devastating devastation; God picks up a phrase Job used in chapter 30 in his dismissive comments about people with whom he shouldn't be compared. The falling of rain in areas that one would dismiss as useless produces a great crop of grass where it is no use to anyone.

God for the first time makes a point that will recur. The world is not organized to suit only humanity. Once again one can make a comparison with Genesis 1, where God does not create humanity until the last afternoon of the week's work. The world does not exist for the sake of humanity; humanity exists for the sake of the world. As Genesis 2 puts it, humanity is created to look after God's garden. In Job 38, the rain does not fall in patterns designed to suit humanity but in patterns designed to suit God's world. A presupposition of Job's attitude has been that the world revolves around him and his happiness; a theme of God's response is that he is mistaken.

The third paragraph concerns the stars and planets. Yet again, they naturally appear in other Old Testament descriptions of creation, but especially in the context of other peoples' belief that the stars and planets determined what happens on earth. In Middle Eastern culture and religion they are very important, and there is a half-truth in that belief about them (Genesis 1 and Isaiah 40 imply): they are under **Yahweh's** control, and they are means of Yahweh's will being implemented in the world. At the most basic level they govern the seasons and tell people when to celebrate festivals. Job cannot control them and thus control what happens in the world; Yahweh can and does.

Yahweh returns to the fact that similarly Job cannot control when it rains. It would be a monumental asset to be able to do so. People could then ensure that they got rain when they needed it: first to soften the ground that has been solidified by the heat of summer and needs breaking up before the cycle of plowing and planting can begin and then to water the crops when they are actively growing. Being able to control the rain would allow people to put an end to the vicious cycle of drought, crop failure, and famine. But they cannot do so. It's not the way God has arranged the world. The point about the reference to the ibis and the cockerel is that they sometimes seemed able to announce the coming of rain—more consistently, the cockerel knows when dawn is imminent. These birds are more knowledgeable than human beings. That deepens human frustration at not being in control of what happens in the world or not being able to understand what happens.

Job has found suffering happening to him in an apparently random way. His friends have denied that it is random; Job is somehow to blame for what has happened to him. God will make explicit in a moment that his friends are wrong in saying Job is responsible for what has happened to him, but God implies that neither is it merely random, any more than what happens in nature is random. God is in control of what happens. Job is wrong to assume that he has the right or opportunity to know the basis on which God acts. One of the book's delicious ironies is that back at the beginning it gave a perfectly good explanation for what has happened to Job (well, you may or may not think it is a perfectly good explanation, but at least it is an explanation), which God could have given Job at this point. One can imagine the conversation. Instead of storming at Job, God could have said, "Right, Job, I will tell you what has been going on . . . ," and Job might (or might not) have said, "Oh, I see; that's okay, then." But God does not do so. One significance of that fact is that Job has to live with his experience the same way as we do, and the book's challenge to us is to live in the way God challenges Job—to submit to God even though we do not know the rationale for what God does.

JOB 38:39–39:30

The Mysteries of Nature

³⁹ Can you hunt prey for the lion
    and satisfy the appetite of the great lions,
⁴⁰ when they crouch in dens,
    lie in wait in a thicket?
⁴¹ Who prepares its provision for the raven
    when its young cry for help to God
    and wander without food?

^{39:1} Do you know the season for the mountain goats to give
    birth,
    watch over the deer's going into labor?
² Do you count the months they complete,
    or do you know the season of their giving birth?
³ They crouch so that they may deliver their young;
    they dismiss their pains.
⁴ Their offspring become strong, they grow up in the open;
    they leave and do not come back to them.

⁵ Who lets the wild donkey go free;
    who loosens the ropes of the wild mule,

⁶ whose home I made the steppe;
    his dwelling, the salt land?
⁷ He scorns the noise of the town;
    he does not listen to the shouts of a driver.
⁸ He ranges the mountains as his pasture
    and searches for any green thing.

⁹ Is the wild ox willing to serve you;
    will it lodge by your feeding trough?
¹⁰ Can you hold the wild ox with a harness to the furrow;
    will he till the valleys behind you?
¹¹ Can you rely on him because his strength is great
    and leave your toil to him?
¹² Can you trust him to bring back your seed
    and gather it to your threshing floor?

¹³ The wing of the ostrich rejoices
    (is it a stork's wing and plumage?),
¹⁴ because she leaves her eggs on the earth,
    lets them get warm on the dirt,
¹⁵ and puts out of mind that a foot may crush them
    or a wild creature trample them.
¹⁶ She is tough with her offspring so that they are not hers,
    without fear that her toil will be in vain,
¹⁷ because God made her forget insight,
    did not allot any understanding to her.
¹⁸ At the time when she flaps on high,
    she scorns the horse and its rider.

¹⁹ Do you give the horse his strength;
    do you clothe his neck with a mane,
²⁰ do you make him quiver like a locust?—
    the majesty of his snort is a terror.
²¹ They paw with force;
    he rejoices with might as he goes out to meet the weapons.
²² He scorns at fear, does not get afraid,
    does not turn back from the sword.
²³ By him rattles a quiver,
    a flashing spear and scimitar.
²⁴ With shaking and excitement he stamps the earth,
    and he cannot stand still when there is the sound of
        the horn.

²⁵ At the blast of the horn he says, "Hey,"
    and from afar he smells battle,
    the thunder of the officers, and the shout.

²⁶ Is it by your understanding that the hawk takes flight,
    spreads his wings to the south?
²⁷ Is it at your word that the eagle soars,
    and that he builds his nest high,
²⁸ dwells on the crag and lodges
    on an outcrop of the crag, a stronghold?
²⁹ From there he looks carefully for food;
    from afar his eyes look out,
³⁰ so his young drink blood;
    where the slain are, there is he.

Often the first thing I hear in the morning is the squawking of a group of parrots who wander around our city, the descendants (says the urban legend) of pet birds that escaped from or were released by their owners. When I sit at my desk, I see squirrels foraging for nuts, and possibly blue jays bathing in a fountain. If I go for a walk in our block's grounds, I may see two mallards that stray here from a pond a little way away. In the evening, a skunk occasionally wanders across our patio. Before bedtime the other night, I killed a black widow spider in the closet. At any time in the kitchen I may realize we have been invaded by ants. I think of our city as signifying a claim that the area belongs to humanity, but the forebearers of most of these creatures were present even before the Chumash Indians arrived, let alone the Europeans.

Yahweh's address to Job continues to remind him that as a human being he is not the center of the animate world. It exists in its own right. God is the one who provides for lions and ravens. Whereas human beings in a traditional culture know all about domesticated goats and sheep, provide for them, and watch over their birthing, it is God who watches over the birthing and maturing of wild goats and deer. It is God who provides a home in the steppe for the wild donkey and provides for the wild ox. Whereas domesticated donkeys and oxen are of crucial importance to humanity, wild donkeys are useless because they won't become subservient to human need, but they are still significant members of the animate world, and God provides for them. The ostrich is an even odder creature. It is a bird, but its wings don't enable it to fly properly, though it can run extraordinarily fast. It lays eggs but (according to legend) does not look after them properly so that its laying becomes fruitful. It seems a silly creature, yet God made it as it is, with its exotic characteristics. The horse is an animal you have to take seriously. In Old Testament times it was not a domesticated animal in the regular sense but one more likely to be associated with warfare; it was kings who had horses. The hawk and the eagle are more accomplished and wise than the ostrich; as God is behind the quirkiness of the ostrich, God is behind the skill of these soaring birds.

One implication of God's portrait of these creatures is that they both do and do not make sense. The lion has to work hard to find food; even more explicitly does the raven, whose young cry out for sustenance. For wild animals, birthing may be painful, as it is for other creatures, and so is the process of nurturing—you bring them up, then they go and never come back (we talk about the empty nest syndrome). The wild donkey has to search far and wide for fodder. The ostrich goes about motherhood in that rather poignant fashion. As well as finding food, the hawk and the eagle have to find refuge for themselves. Yet God is involved in the lives of all the creatures, even though to Job they may not make sense. So perhaps God is involved in caring for Job; perhaps God will provide when Job cries out, even if not immediately; perhaps God does watch as Job goes through his pain; perhaps God is involved with situations that make no human sense; perhaps God understands situations that make no human sense; perhaps God is in control of massive realities that Job cannot control; perhaps God provides protection for beings that would otherwise be hopelessly vulnerable.

God does not draw these inferences for Job. God does not thereby fall into the trap of giving answers, like the friends. Job thinks he wants answers, but in practice the answers that people give sufferers usually fail to satisfy the sufferer in the way they satisfy the comforter. To be truthful, satisfying the comforter is what they are designed to do, because the comforter does not feel comfortable without answers. Much of the time what we need (not what we think we need) is the capacity to live with questions. At one level this is what God wants for Job, that he should be able to live with trust in God when he has no answers.

The answers that are useful to us are often the ones we ourselves come to, and another implication of God's not drawing inferences is that they will benefit Job only if he comes to them himself. In this sense the book of Job parallels the book of Jonah, which closes with a question. The person who listens to the story has to answer it and then think about its implications. The book of Job once again functions in a way that Jesus' parables will follow. As Jesus finishes a story, one can imagine his hearers scratching their heads and asking, "What was that about?" Sometimes the Gospels tell us that this was his disciples' reaction. This way of speaking avoids making the message too plain to people who are unwilling or not ready to receive it.

Jesus' own point in Mark 4 is that telling parables is an act of judgment on people: he speaks in this way so that they will not understand. His presupposition is that they do not want to understand, and his indirect act of judgment is to stop sharing his good news with them. Here, God will go on to reprimand Job. Is God deliberately puzzling Job with his account of creation? Of course Jesus' hearers are free to prove him wrong, and if they are unable to resist turning over his stories in their mind, and then get it, and then turn and believe—Jesus will have achieved his real purpose. The same will apply to God in relation to Job.

JOB 40:1–24

When Silence Is Not Enough

¹ Yahweh replied to Job:
² Does the person who contends with Shadday correct him?—
   The one who reproves God must answer.

³ Job replied to Yahweh:
⁴ No, I am of little account, what could I answer?—
   I put my hand to my mouth.

⁵ I have spoken once, and I will not reply—
  twice, and I will not do so again.

⁶ Yahweh replied to Job from the tempest:
⁷ Fasten on your armor like a man, will you,
  so that I can ask you and you can inform me.
⁸ Would you indeed annul my decision making,
  say that I am in the wrong so that you may be in the right?
⁹ Do you have an arm like God's,
  and can you thunder with a voice like his?

¹⁰ Will you adorn yourself with eminence and grandeur,
  cloth yourself in splendor and majesty,
¹¹ scatter about your angry fury,
  see every eminent person and bring him low,
¹² see every eminent person and make him bow down,
  throw down the faithless where they stand,
¹³ bury them in the dirt all together,
  conceal their faces in the hidden place—
¹⁴ and I too will confess you,
  that your right hand can bring deliverance to you.

¹⁵ There, now, is Behemoth,
  whom I made along with you, who eats grass like cattle.
¹⁶ There, now, his strength is in his loins,
  his power in the muscles of his insides.
¹⁷ He hangs his tail like a cedar;
  the sinews of his thighs are intertwined.
¹⁸ His bones are like tubes of bronze;
  his limbs are like a bar of iron.
¹⁹ He is the first of God's ways;
  his maker can draw near with his sword.
²⁰ Because the mountains bring him produce,
  and all the animals of the wild play there,
²¹ he lies down underneath the lotus plants,
  in the cover of the reeds and in the marsh.
²² The lotus plants screen him as his shade;
  the willows of the wash surround him.
²³ There—when the river gushes, he does not rush;
  he is confident that Jordan bursts forth at his word.
²⁴ Can someone take him by his eyes
  or pierce his nose with traps?

Over the years during which my first wife had multiple sclerosis, I have concrete memories concerning two or three occasions when I attempted to confront God about it. Distressed at the way the illness affected her, on one such occasion I remember saying, "I don't really trust you with Ann," and I remember sensing that God responded by saying, "Would you trust you with Ann if you were me?" (Answer: probably not.) On another such occasion I remember protesting at the way it seemed that her illness would be making it harder for her to relate to God, and I sensed God responding, "How Ann and I relate is between her and me, so shut up."

In much more frightening fashion Job, too, has found that the great but also solemn thing about confronting God is that God may respond and may take as confrontational a stance as we do. Our relationship with God is not so different from our relationship with a human person (surprise, surprise). We may be confident about the way to look at a situation but then find the other person looking at it quite differently and putting our way of thinking into a broader context. It doesn't mean we were totally wrong, but neither were we as right as we thought. And the closer our relationship with the other person, the more confrontational the response may be. In other words, the forceful nature of God's response to Job is not a sign of the relationship's shallowness but of its maturity, about which we know from the beginning of the book.

Yahweh's opening words form the conclusion to his questioning over the past two chapters, and these words themselves appropriately take the form of a question. Job has been contending with Yahweh like a human being bringing a case against another human being. He has been correcting Yahweh. The collection of questions that Yahweh has posed implicitly constituted Yahweh's response to the case and the attempted correction, and therefore Job has to answer them. Way back in chapter 9, Job had commented that contending with God would be impossible; God would simply not respond. You can't act tough with God and come out whole. While he has since spoken further about contending, it has been in terms of God's contending with him, not his contending with God.

Yet contending with God, trying to put God on trial, is pretty much what he has been doing, and God calls him on the matter. Likewise, any talk about correction has concerned God's correction of Job (or Job's correcting his friends), not Job's correction of God, and of course the proper direction of correcting is from teacher or parent to pupil or child, not vice versa. Yet God can reasonably suggest that in substance Job has been correcting God in making points about how God runs the world and about God's claims about how the world works. God's questions have been his response to the contending and the correcting, and now God himself wants some answers.

Job's response is not to provide answers but to do what he said he would do back in chapter 9: even though he was in the right, he would not answer God but ask for grace and mercy. Likewise in chapter 13 he had said that if God were to contend with him, he would be quiet. So here his response to God is simply to give in and forfeit the opportunity to answer God's challenges on the grounds of his being of little significance. One might have thought that this ploy would work well, but when he also made that statement back in chapter 13, he said that he would answer if God summoned him, and in effect God takes him up on this proposition. It is also characteristic of human relationships that when we try to get out of an argument by merely saying, "Yes, you were right," this admission may not take the steam out of the altercation. Job finds that the voice from the tempest continues to speak. I like to imagine Job thinking that his submission will bring to an end the confrontation that he no longer wishes for, now that God has put him in his place, and to imagine his heart sinking as he hears God start up again.

When Job spoke about asking for grace in chapter 9, he described God as "the one who makes decisions about me." Here, God is not clear that Job's submission is more than a mere acknowledgment of God's superior firepower as a debater. Job has certainly not questioned whether God's decision-making power is a reality; he has frequently acknowledged it. But he has questioned the way God exercises that authority. Once more, it was back in chapter 9 that he laid himself open to

God's challenge in this connection. There he recognized that no one can force God to meet with him to discuss God's decision making, and he voiced the suspicion that even if he could get a meeting with God, it would somehow end up with his pleading guilty even though he is actually innocent. In chapter 19 he complained that nobody made a decision in response to his calls for help; by implication, it was God who was failing to exercise his authority. In chapter 22 Job implied that God's decision making is random. It's not unreasonable for God to suggest that Job wants to annul God's decision making in connection with Job himself and in other connections; it looks as if Job thinks he could do better than God.

God's reaction is not to question whether Job has the moral insight to make better decisions than God but to question whether he has the capacity to implement such decisions. "Go on, then, Job," in effect God says. The question is whether Job has an arm like God's to wield a weapon against the faithless, whether Job can roar like God as he charges into battle against the faithless. The people that need putting down are people in power, people in positions of eminence and majesty; does Job have the majesty to stand up to them? Does Job have the kind of capacity for well-directed anger that God has? The story so far has noted that anger exercised by human beings is usually a negative quality but also that anger exercised by God is a different matter; it is an important source of the energy in doing the right thing. Does Job have enough of that kind of anger when confronted by the faithless?

Pointing Job to Behemoth puts flesh on the point. The word *behemoth* is an enhanced version of the Hebrew word for an animal and apparently suggests a giant animal. If we are to identify it as an actual animal, then it will be a creature such as the hippopotamus, but its significance is as an embodiment or symbol of massive strength. Obviously Job cannot hope to tame or control such a creature, but it is one of the creatures God made along with Job. Indeed, God goes on to note, it is the first of God's creatures. Whether this means it came first chronologically or that it is the preeminent creature, it is under God's control. God wields the sword, and it does what God says.

JOB 41:1–34

Leviathan

1 Can you pull in Leviathan with a fishhook
  or tie down his tongue with a rope?
2 Can you put a cord in his nose
  or pierce his jaw with a hook?
3 Will he make many prayers for grace to you;
  will he speak smooth words to you?
4 Will he seal a covenant with you
  so that he is taken as a lifelong servant?
5 Will you play with him like a bird
  or put him on a leash for your girls?
6 Will merchants barter over him;
  will they divide him up among the dealers?
7 Can you fill his skin with harpoons
  or his head with fishing spears?
8 Lay your hand on him;
  be mindful of the battle; don't do it again.
9 There: hope in connection with him deceives itself—
  isn't one overwhelmed at the sight of him?
10 No one is so fierce that he arouses him;
  so who stands up to me?
11 Who confronts me so that I pay?
  —under the whole
  heaven, things are mine.

12 I will not be silent about his limbs
  or his powerful word or the grace of his frame.
13 Who has stripped off the surface of his garment;
  who can come with a double bridle for him?
14 Who can open the doors of his face?—
  his teeth all around are a terror.
15 His row of shields are his pride,
  shut up with a tight seal.
16 One touches the other;
  a breath could not come between them.
17 They stick one to another;
  they clasp each other and cannot separate from each other.
18 His sneezes flash lightning;
  his eyes are like the eyelids of dawn.

¹⁹ From his mouth go torches;
    sparks of fire escape.
²⁰ From his nostrils smoke comes out,
    like a pot heated or [burning] rushes.
²¹ His breath ignites coals;
    flame comes out from his mouth.
²² In his neck strength lodges;
    dismay leaps before him.
²³ The folds of his flesh stick;
    it is cast on him, it does not move.
²⁴ His mind is cast like stone,
    cast like a bottom millstone.
²⁵ At his rising up, divine beings are in dread;
    at his crashing, they fail.
²⁶ The sword that reaches him does not prevail—
    spear, dart, or lance.
²⁷ He counts iron as straw,
    bronze as rotten wood.
²⁸ Arrow does not make him flee;
    sling stones turn into chaff to him.
²⁹ Clubs count as chaff;
    he scorns the shaking of a scimitar.
³⁰ His underparts are sharp bits of pot;
    he spreads a threshing sledge on the mud.
³¹ He makes the deep boil like a pot;
    he makes the sea like a pot of ointment.
³² Behind him he lightens a path;
    one would think the deep to be white hair.
³³ There is no one on the land to rule him,
    made without fear.
³⁴ He sees everything majestic;
    he is king over all noble creatures.

My wife is a bit apprehensive about monsters and can occasionally be scared for a moment by a shadow that might be some strange creature. For our honeymoon she was nevertheless keen to go to Scotland, from where her ancestors came, even though Scotland is also the land of the Loch Ness Monster. It is said that in 1933, the year of the modern discovery of the legendary sea-serpent-like creature, the Secretary of State for Scotland ordered the police to prevent any attacks on it. But reports of the creature go back to the sixth century, when a man was allegedly attacked and killed by it. It then also threatened to attack one of Saint Columba's followers; Columba made the sign of the cross and commanded the creature to halt—which it did. It is the kind of story that is told about saints, which illustrates the way in which strange creatures, and especially strange sea creatures, have long been symbols of frightening and threatening power.

In the Middle Eastern world, Leviathan is one of these. Whereas there are creatures in Middle Eastern stories that remind one of Behemoth, there is no creature that has a similar name, whereas a mythical creature with a name similar to Leviathan appears in a Canaanite story. Both are figures that symbolize extraordinary and frightening negative power. The account of Leviathan owes something to the crocodile, as the account of Behemoth owes something to the hippopotamus, but it would be an oversimplification to equate them. Rather, scholars in the Middle East in ancient times thought of the most powerful, frightening, uncontrollable creatures they could and invited people to picture the power that encouraged disorder and turmoil in the world as an enhanced version of such creatures. They then affirmed that these powers were not actually out of control; their power was under divine constraint.

Elsewhere in the Old Testament, Leviathan appears in Psalm 74, where **Yahweh** is the one who crushed the heads of Leviathan. The psalm speaks in a way that could make people think both of creation and of the deliverance of Israel at the Red Sea, each of them occasions when God broke the back of resistant powers. In contrast, Isaiah 27 promises that God is going to put down Leviathan "in that day," the day when God brings about the consummation of his purpose. That fits with the way Job 3 has already spoken of people who are ready to rouse Leviathan. In addition, Job 7 has referred to the sea and to the dragon, and Job 9 has referred to Rahab, other ways of conceptualizing the same reality. On the other hand, Psalm 104 describes God as creating Leviathan to play in the ocean. Part of what is going on when the Old Testament refers to Leviathan is that it is declaring, "You know the Canaanites say that one of their gods defeated Leviathan? Well, I will tell you who really did so, and when he did it."

These varying references to Leviathan help us to get the kind of complex picture that we need of God's sovereignty over evil. God put evil down at creation (how there came to be evil that God had to deal with way back then is not a question the Bible answers) and in delivering Israel from Egypt, which becomes a kind of embodiment of Leviathan. For that reason there is a sense in which we need not take its threatening nature too seriously; we can smile at it. But experience shows that God did not put down evil in such a way as to make evil totally incapable of asserting itself; it may be constrained, but it is not eliminated. Hence the promise that God will one day complete its subjugation. (Oddly, we might think, the picture of the adversary, the *satan*, in the opening of Job does not correspond to the picture of Satan in later Jewish writings and in the New Testament, but the picture of Leviathan comes much closer to doing so. In other words, Leviathan in the Old Testament corresponds to Satan in the New Testament.)

God's challenge to Job takes a coherent place within this outline. You could say that evil is a little like a powerful creature that God has put on a leash. Its power is constrained but not eliminated. Again, why God should have put evil on a leash rather than simply destroying evil is not a question that the Bible deals with, though we may be able to guess at answers. When human irresponsibility causes terrible catastrophe, why does God not prevent it? Maybe part of the explanation is that it would destroy the reality of human responsibility. We noted in connection with chapter 12 that God did not make the world as a place where we simply relax and enjoy ourselves but as a place where we grow to maturity by accepting responsibility for our actions. Our having to deal with evil (by turning from it) fulfills a similar function. Yet the Bible does not make this point (it is the kind of theory Elihu might have expounded), and one of the points of the book of Job is to discuss the issues raised by our living in a world where we do not have answers to the question "Why do bad things happen to good people?"

We know why bad things happened to Job, but the book of Job presupposes that his story is not everyone's story, which may link with the fact that God never tells Job about the background and purpose behind his experience. While this knowledge might have been helpful to Job, revealing it to him would not have been so helpful to us. Giving us insight on how to live without knowing why things happen to us is more helpful. The key is recognizing that God is trustworthy, so we can live in trust and submission to God even when we do not know why bad things happen to us. The chapter about Leviathan plays a role in pushing Job (and thus us) in that direction. It draws attention to the fearsome might of this embodiment of threatening power and invites us to recognize that (a) we cannot control it and (b) God can and does. Those two facts are reason for trust and submission.

Yahweh's two confrontational addresses to Job as a whole, then, seek to establish two points. They point out that Job is not the center of the universe; it does not revolve around him. And they argue that Yahweh does not do too bad a job of controlling forces that resist Yahweh's purpose in the world, and that Job himself could hardly do a better one. Yahweh then leaves him to draw the implications regarding his suffering.

JOB 42:1–17

And They All Lived Happily Ever After

¹ Job replied to Yahweh:
² I acknowledge that you can do anything;
   no plan can be impracticable for you.
³ "Who is this who darkens purpose without knowledge?"—
   thus I told of things that I did not understand,
   wonders beyond me that I did not know.
⁴ "Listen, will you, and I myself will speak;
   I will ask and you can make it known to me."
⁵ I have listened to you with the listening of an ear,
   and now my eye has seen you.
⁶ Therefore I reject
   and relent over dirt and ashes.

⁷After Yahweh had spoken these words to Job, Yahweh said to Eliphaz the Temanite, "My anger has flared against you and your two friends, because you have not spoken to me what is

right, like my servant Job. [8]So now get yourselves seven bulls and seven rams, go to my servant Job, and sacrifice a burnt offering for yourselves. My servant Job can plead for you, because I will show favor to him so as not to bring disgrace on you, because you have not spoken to me what was right, like my servant Job." [9]Eliphaz the Temanite, Bildad the Shuhite, and Zophar the Naamathite went and did as Yahweh told them.

Yahweh showed favor to Job. [10]Yahweh restored Job's fortunes when he pleaded on behalf of his friends. Yahweh increased all that Job had to double. [11]All his brothers and sisters and former acquaintances came and ate a meal with him at his house. They consoled and comforted him for all the trouble that Yahweh had brought on him, and each of them gave him one piece of silver and one gold ring. [12]Yahweh blessed the latter part of Job's life more than the former. He had fourteen thousand sheep, six thousand camels, a thousand yoke of oxen, and a thousand donkeys. [13]He had seven sons, and three daughters—[14]he named the first Jemimah; the second, Keziah; the third, Keren-happuach. [15]There could not be found anywhere in the country women of a beauty like Job's daughters. Their father gave them property along with their brothers. [16]Afterward, Job lived one hundred and forty years, and saw his sons and his grandsons, four generations. [17]Job died old and full of years.

I have often asked people whether they like the ending of the book of Job. The majority do not because it seems unrealistic, in that they know many people who do not have a happy ending to their story in the way that Job does. My own reaction works the logic in the opposite direction. My first wife came to be disabled by multiple sclerosis and died as a result of the illness, and I don't care to think of her story as simply ending in that way. I am glad that I know that her whole person will be renewed on resurrection day, and I am glad that the story of Job ends with Job restored. The very fact that so many people do not have a happy ending to their story is the reason why a story that has a happy ending is important—not because we are avoiding the toughness of the unhappy ending and fooling ourselves but because God is indeed one who brings stories to a happy ending. The Israelites did not know that their family members who died without a happy ending were going to get one on resurrection day, which makes the story's statement of faith in the God of happy endings even more remarkable.

Evidently Job's second concession speech satisfies **Yahweh** in a way that the first did not. The first failed to do so because it was indeed like a concession speech; acknowledging that the other party has won does not imply acknowledging that he or she deserved to win. Really, Job simply acknowledged that God was bigger than he was. God had superior firepower. Here he takes up God's own words about his not having enough insight to hold forth concerning the issues on which he has been pontificating, and he acknowledges that God is right. He acknowledges that the truth is as God has said: God can do what he wishes to do, and God can implement plans that he makes.

Although Job says he has seen God as well as listened to God, the story has not said so. Elsewhere in the Old Testament, speaking of God appearing in a cloud is regularly a way of indicating that God is really present, speaking, and acting but that God is doing so in such a way that you do not see God. We noted in connection with Elihu's promise in Job 33 that seeing God would blind you. God's speaking from the tempest has similarly meant that Job has indeed heard God with his ears but also that he has metaphorically seen God, as Elihu promised. "I'll see you in court," the saying goes, and this has been Job's desire (for instance, in the "I know that my redeemer liveth" passage in chapter 19). In effect, God has met his plea or challenge, but the statement he has made is very different from the kind Job was looking for. Yet its result has been to make Job withdraw his case.

Perhaps it is then his own case that Job "rejects," and thus he repents about the feebleness of his human nature as mere dirt and ashes. The King James Version had him repenting "in" dirt and ashes, but the phrase is one that would usually denote repenting "about" dirt and ashes. Further, while the story has had him sitting "in the midst of the ashes," it was his friends who put dirt on their heads, not Job himself. When the phrase "dirt and ashes" appears in the Old Testament, it is a description of human feebleness and mortality. Dirt is what we start as, and we end up as ashes. Job is thus using the expression in connection with repenting over his pretensions to be able as a mere mortal to get his mind around the issues he has been raising.

Compared with God, Job is lacking in insight, yet God's appearing to him has elicited an acknowledgment of some key truths about God. While Job had implicitly overestimated his own capacity to run the world or understand the issues involved in running the world, he has come to accept his limitations. Compared with his three friends, he is thus a man of understanding—an ironic fact, given how full of themselves his friends have been. Eliphaz and his friends have spoken with confidence about the people who make God angry, yet perhaps it is an occupational hazard for such people to learn that they are people of this kind. God makes no comment about Elihu, who is just as full of himself as the other three but argued points that partially anticipated God's own. There is also no return to the scene in the heavenly cabinet for God to say to the adversary, "I told you so." But there is no doubt that Job has passed his test.

God urges a further reversing of positions between Job and his friends. It would be nice to think that your friends would pray for you when you are in a situation like Job's. Maybe they did so when they lifted their voices, wept, ripped their coats, and threw dirt over their heads to the heavens. Such actions would be the appropriate accompaniment to praying prayers like the ones in the Psalms for a person like Job. But the story never quite says that they prayed, even though they implicitly see Job as the object of God's anger. They are now definitely the objects of God's anger. Neatly, God tells them what to do if they want to get out of being the objects of God's anger— because the restoration of the relationship between God and them requires a move on their part as well as on God's. Simply forgiving them won't achieve that restoration. If they ask Job to make an offering and pray on their behalf, then the relationship can be healed. It's quite an offering, too, and while the Old Testament allows for small-scale offerings by people who can afford no more, these are rich guys. Of course God could have told them to bring their own offering and do their own praying, but getting them to involve Job is a stronger expression of their recognizing that they have been in the wrong and that Job has been in the right. It would also ensure that Job cannot hold on to any justified resentment at the way they have let him down. Resolving issues in life is often incomplete if we only resolve issues between us and God; we also have to make sure that relationships with other people are restored. And there's nothing like praying for someone to make sure your attitude to the person is in order. Thus there turns out to be a link between Job's willingness to pray for his friends and the restoration of Job's own life, which only follows on the prayer. It is in keeping with this idea that Jesus says that we will be forgiven only if we forgive others, and not otherwise.

The nature and the magnitude of Job's restoration may raise an eyebrow or two, and one wonders what Mrs. Job thought about bearing another ten children. Admittedly, the story may well assume (as we noted in connection with Job 31) that a man of Job's stature would be likely to have more than one Mrs. Job, though that may make people in the West feel no better about the story. We would also be aware that ten new children do not cancel out the loss of the first ten. Given that the end of the story is meant to highlight the wonder of God's restoration of Job, we might permit ourselves to allow for Middle Eastern hyperbole and assume we don't have to take the details too literally. On the other hand, the countercultural note about Job's giving property to his daughters means the book (almost) ends with a final testimony to what an extraordinary man Job was, capable of sitting loose to social norms and filled with love and commitment for the daughters of his restored life.

With a final irony in this book full of irony, the story's last scene asserts that the traditional teaching affirmed by the friends and by Job (and subsequently by Jesus) is right. Those who honor God, God honors. Submission to the Lord is insight; turning from evil is understanding. Yet that does not somehow dispose of the questions that the rest of the book has raised. The book has looked at various possible ways of looking at suffering, none of which apply in every case, but all of which may sometimes apply. It began from the possibility that suffering can be a test that reveals whether someone's commitment to God is genuine; both the Old and the New Testament confirm that such testing is a reality of the life of Israel and of the church. Suffering is designed to vindicate the nature of our relationship with God. The book has incorporated the insight of Elihu that when we are suffering, God does reach out to us in love and concern to draw us to him. It has incorporated the urgings of Yahweh to accept the limits to our understanding and power and to trust God even when we cannot understand what God is doing. It has implied the recognition that even when there is an answer to why you suffer, you may never know what it is.

It has incorporated Job's impassioned pleas and protests, which are like those in the Psalms but appear here on a gargantuan scale, suggesting that even though Job ends up having to submit to God on the assumption that God knows better, his stance is nevertheless one that God prefers to that of the friends. A little while ago, a couple I know had a baby who died a few days after he was born. His memorial service incorporated a series of verses from the book of Job that expressed pain and protest, submission and hope. Someone who attended said she would start coming to the church because she did not know another church where these feelings and questions could be voiced.

All these insights about suffering and about how to respond to it need to be part of our awareness, not merely when something terrible happens but before it happens so that they can become resources to us if it does happen. It will be too late then to start trying to work out what attitude we take to suffering. Rather, the experience will bring out how we already think.

In this sense, I doubt whether the book is designed for people who are suffering, though it may help them to know that other people have felt the way they do. Thus maybe when you meet Job or his wife or any of the first ten children or the servants in heaven and you ask them what they thought about what happened to them, they may reply that yes, at the time they felt they had a raw deal, but they now know that so many people have been helped by their story over two and a half millennia that they don't mind having suffered for people in this way, especially as they did have their unexpected resurrection to new life.

Certainly the book is not designed to help us see what to say to a person who is suffering. Indeed, it offers no hint that anyone should have said anything to Job. It implicitly does not think much of what people did say to him, but it does not imply that there are other things that one should say. Perhaps it implies that the best thing is to say nothing. I am not clear that the friends' silence was a good silence, but there is such a thing as a good silence, especially if it is the silence of a listener and a witness, and one that encourages the sufferer to voice the hurt, the questions, and the protests that arise from his or her heart and then does not apply a Band-Aid to it.

GLOSSARY

Abaddon

One of the Old Testament's words for the place where dead people are, like **Sheol**. The ordinary word is similar to a Hebrew word meaning "perish," which may not be a coincidence. Indeed, the verb can suggest "destroy," and people might make a link with the fact that death does mean that our bodies decay. But the texts do not make anything of this. The word is simply a name.

commitment

The word corresponds to the Hebrew word *hesed*, which translations render by means of expressions such as steadfast love or loving-kindness or goodness. The Old Testament uses this word to refer to an extraordinary act of generosity, allegiance, or grace whereby someone pledges himself or herself to someone else when there is no prior relationship between them and therefore no reason why the person should do so. Thus in Joshua 2, Rahab appropriately speaks of her protection of the Israelite spies as an act of commitment. It can also refer to a similar extraordinary act that takes place when there is a relationship between people but one party has let the other party down and therefore has no right to expect any faithfulness from the other. If the party that has been let down continues being faithful, she or he is showing this kind of commitment. In their response to Rahab, the Israelite spies declare that they will relate to her in this way. In the New Testament, the special word for love, *agapē*, is equivalent to *hesed*.

covenant

The Hebrew word *berit* covers covenants, treaties, and contracts, but these are all ways in which people make a formal commitment about something, and I have used the word *covenant* for all three. Where you have a legal system that people can appeal to, contracts assume a system for resolving disputes and administering justice that can be used if people do not keep their commitments. In contrast, a covenantal relationship does not presuppose an enforceable legal framework of that kind, but a covenant does involve some formal procedure that confirms the seriousness of the solemn commitment one party makes to another. Thus the Old Testament often speaks of *sealing* a covenant, literally of *cutting* it (the background lies in the kind of formal procedure described in Genesis 15 and Jeremiah 34:18–20, though such an actual procedure would hardly be required every time someone made a covenantal commitment). People make covenants sometimes *to* other people and sometimes *with* other people. The former implies something more one-sided; the latter, something more mutual.

Shadday

Shadday is a name for God that occurs frequently in Job. We do not know whether the name had a particular meaning. It resembles words meaning mountain, breast, and destruction. The Old Testament occasionally suggests that Shadday is the Destroyer, but generally it does not imply that the word has a particular meaning. Its great frequency in Job likely reflects the sense that it is appropriate on the lips of non-Israelites instead of the name **Yahweh**. The conventional translation "Almighty" derives from the old Greek translation of the Old Testament, the Septuagint.

Sheol

The most frequent of the Hebrew names for the place where we go when we die (see also **Abaddon** and the comments on Job 11). In the New Testament it is called Hades. It is not a place of punishment or suffering but simply a resting place for everyone, a kind of nonphysical analogue to the tomb as a resting place for our bodies.

Torah

The Hebrew word for the first five books of the Bible. They are often referred to as the "Law," but this title gives a misleading impression. Genesis is nothing like "law," and even Exodus to Deuteronomy are not "legalistic" books. The word *torah* itself means "teaching," which gives a clearer impression of the nature of the Torah.

Yahweh

Most English translations often have the word "LORD" in all capitals, and sometimes the word "GOD" in similar format. These represent Yahweh, the name of God. In later Old Testament times, Israelites stopped using the name Yahweh and started to refer to Yahweh as "the Lord." There may be two reasons. They wanted other people to recognize that Yahweh was the one true God, and this strange, foreign-sounding name could give the impression that Yahweh was just Israel's tribal god, whereas "the Lord" was a term anyone could recognize. In addition, they did not want to fall foul of the warning in the Ten Commandments about misusing Yahweh's name. Translations into other languages then followed suit in substituting an expression such as "the Lord" for the name Yahweh. The downsides are that it ignores God's wish to be known by name, that often the text refers to Yahweh and not some other (so-called) god or lord, and that it gives the impression that God is much more "lordly" and patriarchal than God actually is. (The form "Jehovah" is not a real word but a mixture of the consonants of Yahweh and the vowels of the word for "Lord," to remind people in reading Scripture that they should say "the Lord" and not the actual name.)

CPSIA information can be obtained at www.ICGtesting.com
Printed in the USA
LVOW070539250313

325716LV00001B/1/P